The Layman and his Church

MICHAEL ELLIOTT-BINNS

Assistant Secretary to the General Synod

SECOND EDITION

CHURCH INFORMATION OFFICE
CHURCH HOUSE, WESTMINSTER, SW1

ISBN 0 7151 4545 2

First published 1970
Second edition 1974

© Central Board of Finance of the
Church of England 1974

Printed in England by the Church Army Press, Cowley, Oxford

CONTENTS

Foreword

This book is about the Church's organisation and is intended primarily for laymen engaged on this work, though it has also been found helpful by clergymen and others interested. It was first published in 1970 when a new system of government was coming into operation. This is a second edition and has been substantially revised. Quite a lot of water has flowed under the bridge in the last four years.

The new system introduced in 1970 was called 'synodical government' and the Foreword to the first edition began by explaining what this phrase means. 'Government' was seen as a rather unhelpful word, which suggested people ordering other people about. But the Church is a free society based on the recognition of mutual love. Therefore government is primarily self-government, accepting and conforming to a system of order which is true to the situation and the people in it. At once one reacts against statements of this kind. This is idealism, a pipe-dream, and actual experience of living in the system proves it to be so. But the Christian belief in God proclaims the ideal and the real to be one. The system of government chosen must be realistic in the situation, but must also be capable of development into the ideal, so that it does not impede the movement of the Spirit.

In our human situation, government and lack of it, for good or ill, always to some extent for both, are like the poor 'always with us', and like the fact of poverty around us present certain demands upon us, which we either face or fail to face at our peril.

One clear demand upon us is that of choosing the best available system to meet the needs of the present and the foreseeable future. It must derive from the past, because the present and future derive from the past, and to cut oneself off from one's roots is certainly dangerous and probably in practice impossible. But past attitudes must not be allowed to dictate. Development is essential, in a rapidly changing world often rapid development.

In 1969 and 1970 as part of the process of development the Church chose to put into operation the system of synods. Synod derives from two Greek words, one meaning 'with' or 'together' and the other 'road' or 'way'. The Church chose a new way

v

of growing together. We are not to walk alone, each by himself on his own road. Bishops, clergy and laity, parish, deanery, diocese and centre, are all to go forward together. All must understand and support each other.

After choosing a system the second requirement is to operate it effectively. Any system based on the co-operation of diverse elements is bound to be subject to tensions. Tensions are there to be resolved into a harmony that transcends them. Yet in practice different attitudes are hard to reconcile. Attempts at reconciliation cause delay and sometimes either the appearance or reality of waste of time and lack of decision.

The only immediate practical cure for such ills is efficient autocracy, but that is not the Christian answer. God rules and God has chosen to give us freedom to exercise fruitfully. But this does not necessarily mean complete democracy. There are others in the Church and regard is paid to the place of each person in his order as bishop, clergyman or layman, as well as his place as an individual Christian. A balance needs to be struck between the two concepts. So authority and democracy are both elements in the Church's system, but authority, except in extreme circumstances, is based on willing acceptance rather than compulsion.

Besides choosing and operating the system, the third requirement is to keep it under review, having in mind both the need for continuity and the need for development. The system must not be assessed as though it were operating in a vacuum, but must be judged both in relation to current circumstances which are always changing and to the people who work the system. Sometimes criticism of the system may mean antagonism to a particular situation or it may mask a sense of personal inadequacy to meet specific needs. In such cases changes in the system are likely to do more harm than good. The Church's real need is that people should, under God, face their situations and themselves.

Of course the system matters. But the people who work the system matter more. The system matters because it is part of the life of the Church and derives its importance from that life. If a synod works well then it contributes to the life of the Church in the area which it serves. But there are more important things, worshipping God, preaching the gospel, strengthening the Christian fellowship. In comparison law and organisation are rightly regarded as pedestrian. Many Church people should not involve themselves deeply in most of the questions covered by this book and it would be a waste of time for them to read it. Other people, because the organisation of the Church is their special contribution or part of their wider duty or interest, need and want to know. The whole Church relies on them to do this work, and if it is not done or is done badly, then the whole Church suffers. The purpose of this book is to help the work to be done efficiently, quickly and with sensitivity.

Because the system matters, it needs to be kept up to date and improved. The first years of synodical government have revealed various problems. Some require modifications in the system. Others require noting and watching, because it is too soon for a definite judgement leading to a new development. In 1974 and 1975 the first changes of substance in the system will come into operation.

Increasing reliance is being placed upon the laity and there is thus an increasing need that they should be well informed. It is also still true that much the greatest number of lay people have their contact with the Church through the parish in which they live or worship. Yet there is also a growing tendency for groups of Christians to come together outside the parochial structure, because they share a common field of work or common interest. In this way the parochial system is supplemented, but no proposal has been seriously entertained to replace the parish by some other form of local organisation. Although the parish remains and is likely to remain, there is a growing emphasis on parishes co-operating with each other and seeing themselves as part of the wider Church and the wider community. Parishes must not be parochial in the wrong sense.

Another development is the increasing co-operation between the Churches. In the past few years there has been a movement towards giving formal recognition to such co-operation, in addition to the continuing search for unity.

The first edition was written quickly to meet a special need, helping people to understand and operate a new system that was just coming into existence. Even so the attempt was made to set the new system in the context of the life of the Church as a whole. This second edition gives the same kind of practical information, but devotes more space to questions of general Church organisation and possible lines of development. As familiarity with the practical working of the parish grows, so parishioners will be able to increase their understanding of wider issues.

The subject of this book is the Church's own system. Very little is said about the effect of the secular law and changes in it on the Church. This is an enormous field covering such matters as taxation and planning law. To have included it would have much enlarged the book, and would have required skills beyond those possessed by the author. Even in the field of Church law no attempt has been made to give a complete exposition, except where this is necessary for the layman in the parish. Otherwise there is simplification, but it is hoped that this simplification gives a fair outline impression of the whole.

This book is divided into four parts. The first gives a thumbnail sketch of the history and present position of the organisation of the Church and a fuller general account of the parish organisation. The second sets out the synodical government machinery in the parish and does so fully. While the actual rules should be in the possession of those responsible for working the system this account can be regarded as accurate and sufficient. The third part indicates the rather complex law of property holding in the parish and is technical. Professional advice and reference to the actual Measures concerned is essential for those responsible. The fourth part sketches out the law relating to the life of the parish, sometimes fairly fully and sometimes by indication only according to the extent of the concern of the layman in the matters under discussion.

MICHAEL ELLIOTT-BINNS

PART I—BACKGROUND

1. History

The history of any organised society, and the Church is being considered as such, rests on the developing relationship of two needs of man. He needs to be himself. He needs to be part of a community. The Church should insist and usually has always insisted on both needs and its organisation tries to hold them in balance so that they complement each other and are not in conflict. But an organisation is made up of human beings who are inevitably limited and self-centred. Authority stifles the proper expression of human personality and insight. Freedom leads to one harming another for his own ends or the misery of general disorder. Organisation is never anything like perfect in its expression or its operation, but it is a necessary part of proper living.

One begins with the idea of the family, the small group united by ties of blood. The individual relies on his family for survival and is closely identified with it. Families for their increased strength and better living bind themselves together into communities. Communities join in nations and man has the vision of a single society combining all nations in brotherhood.

The idea of that brotherhood is expressed in the Christian vision. All men are children of God, individuals in their own right with their own relationship to him. All men are brothers related to each other, indeed related so closely as to be like parts of a single body. The Church of England came into being as part of the Church universal roughly during the course of the seventh century. For various reasons, doctrinal and social, there has been a tendency towards division in the Church, and the Church of England had a strong individual identity because of its island situation. At the Reformation the Church of England reorganised itself as a separate national Church. It still is, as it always has been, a branch of the Church universal.

Within the Church there has always been the need for the local society. There was the Church in Jerusalem, the Church in the house of a particular leading Christian. As the Church established itself two basic organisations grew up. There is the Church of the people in a community in day to day contact, which in the Church of England became the parish with its parish priest. There is the Church that can be united effectively under the care of a single Christian leader, the diocese with its bishop.

This simple basic system still exists today, but there have been elaborations. Dioceses have combined together and submitted to control within the Church. In England there are the two provinces of Canterbury and York each with its archbishop. Since early mediaeval times each province has had its convocation, which exercised a certain control over the dioceses, particularly by the making of Canons, and also used to tax the clergy.

There was no central ecclesiastical body acting for the whole Church. The King and Parliament exercised a measure of control. Until the Reformation the Pope also had authority, and inevitably conflicts arose. The tendency of the laity would be to support the King against the Pope while the allegiance of the clergy would be uneasily divided.

Within the diocese archdeaconries and rural deaneries were created to assist its administration. Certain churches or places were given a particular status outside the ordinary organisation, of which surviving examples are the cathedrals which have a special relationship with the bishop, Westminster Abbey and St George's Chapel, Windsor, and the Inns of Court.

One important characteristic of the organisation was the close integration of Church and State. Since the reign of Elizabeth I the monarch has been the Supreme Governor of the Church. Parliament has legislated for Church matters in the same way as for other aspects of the life of the nation. Church leaders were often the King's ministers in secular matters, and the clergy being the educated class acted as civil servants.

This seemed perfectly natural because the Church was the Church of the nation and English people were expected to be members of the Church of England. If they were not they could not expect to take part in the government of the country or have the full privileges of citizenship.

In the parish spiritual authority subject to the law and the limited rights of ecclesiastical superiors rested with the incumbent. The vestry and the churchwardens represented the laity of the parish, that is the whole community. This situation is illustrated by the fact that a qualification of Church membership was not attached to the office of churchwarden as it did not occur to anyone that it would be necessary. Both the churchwarden and the vestry had secular functions as well as ecclesiastical.

THE GROWTH OF THE PRESENT ORGANISATION

Between the sixteenth and the early twentieth centuries the life of the Church and nation changed in many ways, but, disregarding the short interlude of the Commonwealth, Church organisation remained much as it had been.

During the nineteenth century however it became obvious that considerable reform would be necessary. A smaller proportion of the population of the country were active Church members. The disabilities of other religious bodies and non-believers were removed. Many public duties that had been carried out by the Church were transferred to other bodies. The life of the Church and the life of the State and the community at large were becoming more separate. One important consequence of this division was the growth of the concept of the faithful layman. Some laymen were members of the Church while others were not. Of those who were members some were active and others were nominal.

During the early years of this century the Church was conscious of two vital needs for her good government. First, it was essential to her health that the faithful laity should play their proper part. Much was already being done on a voluntary basis and the equivalent of what are now known as parochial church councils and deanery and diocesan synods were often to be found. Houses of Laymen had been called in to assist the Convocations and there was a Representative Church Council consisting of the members of both Convocations with their Houses of Laymen. But these new bodies had no legal powers at all and their decisions were without binding force. The second need was for legislative powers. As the life of the Church and the State had been so intimately interwoven nearly every aspect of the Church's life was affected by Acts of Parliament. But now Parliament was growing much busier and had less time for Church affairs, and therefore it was becoming more and more difficult to get Bills through Parliament. So the Church was unable to adjust its machinery to meet the needs of a rapidly changing world.

Between 1919 and 1921 a new and legally binding system of lay representation was set up. Baptised members of the Church could have their names entered on the church electoral roll of their parish and so become entitled to vote in the elections to the parochial church council and other bodies. These councils were given considerable powers of managing property. There must be diocesan conferences and might also be ruri-decanal conferences though these were not made compulsory. The National Assembly of the Church of England (known as the Church Assembly) was set up consisting of the Houses of Bishops and Clergy, whose members were the same as the members of the two Convocations, and the House of Laity elected by the lay members of the diocesan conferences. Lay people serving on these bodies must be communicants. In 1919 Parliament, by the 'Enabling Act', authorised the Church Assembly to pass Measures, which should be laid before both Houses of Parliament, and if both Houses so resolved sent to the Sovereign for the Royal Assent, after which they would have the force of Acts of Parliament. In this way the Church had taken a big step towards a solution of both her problems of government.

But the old system remained alongside the new. Parliament retained its oversight and could veto any Measure of the Church Assembly. In fact this happened four times in the 1920s, including the rejection of the Prayer Book Measures of 1927 and 1928. Since then no Measure has been rejected, but Measures have been withdrawn by the Assembly because an unfavourable reception seemed likely. The Convocations still exercised their power. The churchwardens remained, though the advent of the parochial church councils had taken some of their functions from them. The vestries were not abolished, but in practice most of them never met because they had no duties to perform.

In the last fifty years the Convocations and the Church Assembly have been active and many branches of Church law and

4

administration have been reformed. But until the passing of the Synodical Government Measure only small changes were made in the basic system of government.

In the 1920s an attempt was made to revise the Prayer Book but two Measures were rejected by Parliament. Since then there was a reluctance to legislate on the spiritual and doctrinal sides of the life of the Church. But just before the Second World War the Convocations decided to revise the Code of Canons. This dated from 1603–4 though there had been a few additions and modifications since then. All kinds of questions have arisen and required solution. It was found that the procedure was clumsy. The two Convocations of Canterbury and York had to consult together. Also it became very apparent that the laity had no place in the revision unless a Measure was required to authorise a particular Canon. The House of Laity of the Church Assembly was consulted as a matter of grace, and this led to further procedural delays and consultations. There were other matters which were not legally the concern of the laity, doctrinal questions, relations with other Churches.

The debate on the issue of what has become known as synodical government, by which is meant participation of bishops, clergy and laity in decision making over the whole field of the Church's concern, began in the Church Assembly in 1953. It ended with the implementation of the Synodical Government Measure in 1969–70 The time taken and the many committees, reports and debates, in the Convocations, the Church Assembly and the dioceses, are evidence of the need for reform.

The Church Assembly was renamed and reconstituted as the General Synod, and the Convocations transferred their functions to the General Synod. However they remained in being and can now exercise some of their former functions in their own provinces. The Houses of Bishops, Clergy and Laity of the General Synod have full authority over all Church matters, though in doctrinal matters the special position of the Bishops is preserved.

Early in the discussions on synodical government there were those who recognised that a new central organisation could only operate effectively if it was backed by a more coherent and efficient system at diocesan and deanery level, so that there could be proper and orderly communication from centre to parish and back again.

5

Diocesan synods have been established and much thought was given to deanery synods which replace the ruri-decanal conferences. These had a somewhat uncertain existence and were indeed under the previous law optional and not essential.

The idea of synodical government began at the centre and moved outwards. Only at the last stages were the implications for the parish worked out. The organisation here was not much altered, but the relationship between the incumbent and the parochial church council was changed to encourage closer co-operation.

In 1969 the new Canons also came into operation. These made many changes in Church organisation and in particular authorised greater flexibility in the services of the Church and increased participation of the laity. A number of changes have been made in the position and duties of clergymen and laymen in the parish in other respects.

A third major piece of legislation passed at that time was the Pastoral Measure 1968. This authorised new kinds of parochial organisations and a wider use of buildings for worship other than the traditional parish church.

The General Synod during its four and a half years of life has taken up many subjects and has made considerable progress in them, more progress more quickly than would have been possible in the time of the Church Assembly and the Convocations. Much of its work is inherited from them, but much it has itself initiated. There are sometimes complaints that it is impossible to deal properly with all the business that comes up. Careful time-tabling is necessary, perhaps involving deliberate delay. The Church must have time to discover its mind. Sometimes consultation with the diocesan synods is necessary or desirable.

This book is concerned with the organisation of the Church, and some discussions and decisions in the Synod, including some of the most important ones, are outside its scope.

The most important constitutional change is probably the Church of England (Worship and Doctrine) Measure. At the time of writing the Measure still has to have final Synod approval and parliamentary approval before Royal Assent can be given. It increases the authority of the Church to reach decisions on worship and doctrine without the need to go to Parliament. The

6

Synod has also considered general questions relating to the worship of the Church, has approved Series 3 Holy Communion, and has begun discussing the principles of baptism, confirmation and marriage. It has prepared a new declaration of assent to the doctrine and worship of the Church to be taken by clergymen and some laymen when taking up offices.

The Synod has defined the relationship of the Church of England with the Churches of North India and Pakistan and approved a closer relationship with the Church of South India. It decided that the time was not ripe for a scheme of reunion with the Methodist Church, but has entered upon new discussions with the other Churches in England on the initiative of the newly established United Reformed Church. It has authorised communicant members of other Churches to communicate at Church of England services.

Besides making modifications in the system of synodical government, the Synod has begun discussions on the method of appointing bishops, the place of episcopacy in the life of the Church and the size of dioceses. It has continued discussion of the ministry following upon *The Paul Report* and *Partners in Ministry*, and has commissioned legislation on the offices of clergy and their stipends and has passed legislation on a new system for the repair of parsonages houses. It has discussed but not yet reached conclusions on the proper method of appointing clergymen to livings. It has begun debating the question of the ordination of women and has gone some way in reorganising the theological colleges.

So work is in progress over most of the field of Church organisation, and when final decisions are reached and implemented there should be changes made that will help the Church to face the problems of the seventies more effectively.

2. The Church

How can one describe the Church of England? This book is about the Church as an institution, about its laws and rules. It is therefore quite inadequate as a description. The Church of England is fundamentally about love, love of God first, and love of one's neighbour second. Its field of operation is England but its field of concern is wider, the world, and wider still, heaven as well as earth, or perhaps better heaven and earth seen together as a single whole.

But still it is an institution with rules, because it needs rules to sustain it. They should be the right rules to further the work and not hinder it, but the rules are subordinate. You cannot express life in rules. The family is an obvious parallel. There is a certain amount of family law, usually governing what happens when things go wrong. If things are going right you do not need laws. Each family has to have rules. There must be a certain time of getting up so that father catches his train to the office and the children get to school and mother sees that these necessary events happen. But rules should be limited in number and reasonably flexible. When I was young my family ate at seven in the evening. Absence except for special reason explained in advance was unthinkable. Lateness was a nuisance and a misdemeanour which might be excused or forgiven. This was carrying a rule too far for the good of family life. Today members of some families seem to roll up when they like and grab what food there is. This may well be worse and more destructive.

The Church needs rules. The Church of England probably has too many and some are probably not right for the present time. There is a tremendous task of rethinking and reordering and this is being undertaken. The Church is also frequently under criticism. Some of it is based on a profound misunderstanding of what the Church is there for. It is often regarded as a social welfare organisation existing for the convenience and comfort of the people of England. If you happen to be interested in society and have no strong conviction about or interest in God, this is a natural reaction. But just as one cannot fairly comment

8

on a person, unless one knows him and has the respect and love for him that should come from knowledge, so comments on the Church are only helpful if they are based on an understanding both of its place in society and its eternal mission. If one goes deeply into the organisation of the Church of England, apparent defects of substance or language may be found to embody realities that ought not to be swept away, but very likely require reinterpretation

Only a rough sketch can be given in this chapter and there is inevitably some blurring of detail. Also no attempt is made to give more than general references to sources.

DOCTRINE AND WORSHIP

The Code of Canons passed from 1964 to 1969 goes some way towards describing what the Church of England is. The first section is headed ' Of the Church of England '.

It ' belongs to the true and apostolic Church of Christ '. Its doctrine is ' grounded in the holy Scriptures and in such teachings of the ancient Fathers and Councils of the Church as are agreeable to the said Scriptures. In particular such doctrine is to be found in the Thirty-nine Articles of Religion, the Book of Common Prayer and the Ordinal '. The Church, under a Measure of 1965, has been engaged in experimenting with forms of worship, though such forms must be ' neither contrary to nor indicative of any departure from the doctrine of the Church of England '. Subject to the same safeguard special forms of service may be authorised, or a clergyman can make minor deviations from the Prayer Book Services or compose services of his own for special occasions. The power to authorise experimental forms of service to be used in place of those in the Prayer Book ends in 1980.

This is the law as it stands at present, but documents have been approved by the General Synod which further define and develop the Church's approach to doctrine and worship.

The form of the Church of England (Worship and Doctrine) Measure has been settled by the Synod, but it requires approval by Parliament before it can receive the Royal Assent and come into operation. It is the result of a report on Church and State published in 1970. An earlier version of the Measure was put to all diocesan synods and there was overwhelming support for it.

On doctrine the Measure provides that decisions taken under it must be neither contrary to, nor indicative of any departure from the doctrine of the Church of England in any essential matter. This formula at once ensures faithfulness to what is unchanging and yet authorises development where this is appropriate in the light of changing circumstances and increasing knowledge.

On worship the Measure replaces existing law including the Act of Uniformity, which requires the use of the Book of Common Prayer, and the 1965 Measure. It will be considered in greater detail in Chapter 10. Here it is sufficient to say that the main change is the giving of authority to the General Synod to approve forms of service alternative to those in the Book of Common Prayer for indefinite use. The services in the Book of Common Prayer must remain available for parishes that wish to use them. There is no time limit on the use of this power. A series of Canons which will bring the system into full effect is already prepared.

The Measure also permits the General Synod to authorise by Canon law forms of the declaration of assent which clergymen take on ordination and entering into office and which is also taken by deaconesses, readers and lay judges in Church courts. The present form which is contained in an Act of 1865 reads as follows:

' I, *A.B.,* do solemnly make the following declaration: I assent to the Thirty-nine Articles of Religion, and to the Book of Common Prayer and of the Ordering of Bishops, Priests, and Deacons. I believe the doctrine of the Church of England as therein set forth to be agreeable to the Word of God; and in public prayer and administration of the sacraments I will use the form in the said book prescribed and none other, except so far as shall be ordered by lawful authority.'

A Canon has been prepared which sets out a new form of the declaration together with a preface to be spoken by the person to whom the clergyman or layman makes the declaration. As the question of the doctrine of the Church is important both are set out:

' PREFACE '

The Church of England is part of the One, Holy, Catholic and Apostolic Church worshipping the one true God, Father, Son and Holy Spirit. She professes the faith uniquely revealed in the Holy Scriptures and set forth in the catholic creeds, which faith the Church is called upon to proclaim afresh in each generation. Led by the Holy Spirit, she has borne witness to Christian truth in her historic formularies, the Thirty-nine Articles of Religion, the Book of Common Prayer and the Ordering of Bishops, Priests and Deacons. In the declaration you are about to make will you affirm your loyalty to this inheritance of faith as your inspiration and guidance under God in bringing the grace and truth of Christ to this generation and making Him known to those in your care?

DECLARATION OF ASSENT

I, *A.B.*, do so affirm, and accordingly declare my belief in the faith which is revealed in the Holy Scriptures and set forth in the catholic creeds and to which the historic formularies of the Church of England bear witness; and in public prayer and administration of the sacrament, I will use only the forms of service which are authorised or allowed by Canon.'

This form of words binds the declarer to the spirit of the historic formularies but not in all respects to their letter. Inevitably through the passage of time there is the occasional sentence in the Prayer Book and the Thirty-nine Articles which gives rise to difficulties for the Christian today. What seems remarkable to many of us, considering how long ago they were written, is how few these sentences are.

RELATIONS WITH OTHER CHURCHES

The last of the Canons in the section on the Church of England reads as follows:—

' Forasmuch as the Church of Christ has for a long time past been distressed by separations and schisms among Christian men, so that the unity for which our Lord prayed is impaired and the witness to his gospel is grievously hindered, it is the duty of clergy and people to do their utmost not only to avoid occasions of strife but also to seek in penitence and brotherly charity to heal such divisions.'

11

The Church of England being part of ' the true and apostolic Church of Christ ' looks forward to a future in which the unity of that Church is better expressed than at present. This will mean, not the destruction of the Church of England, but its merging into a wider entity.

The Church of England is part of the Anglican Communion, a group of Churches which shares the same faith and order. There are provinces, dioceses and congregations of the Anglican Communion in practically every part of the world. Elsewhere, such as parts of Europe and of South America there are Anglican dioceses which do not form part of any province. There are now three united Churches which include former dioceses of the Anglican Communion. They are the Churches of South India, North India and Pakistan. The Church of England is now in communion with all three.

As President of the Lambeth Conference, the Archbishop of Canterbury has a special position in the Anglican Communion, but his jurisdiction outside England is limited to some extra-provincial dioceses, although in some provinces, such as that of South Africa, his services are retained as an ultimate Court of Appeal in certain areas. The Lambeth Conference of bishops normally meets every ten years. The last Conference in 1968 set up the Anglican Consultative Council of bishops, clergy and laity representing the Anglican Churches. This has met twice at Limuru in 1971 and Dublin in 1973. The decisions both of the Lambeth Conference and of the Consultative Council are of persuasive force but they do not bind the Churches.

The Church of England has special relationships with Churches outside the Anglican Communion, such as the Old Catholics and the Scandinavian Churches. It is seeking closer relationships with other Churches in this country but there are difficulties in working out concrete schemes, and in 1969 a scheme for reunion with the Methodist Church just failed to win a sufficient measure of acceptance to be put into operation. A similar scheme was put a second time to the General Synod in 1971 and again did not win a sufficient majority. In 1972 however the Congregational Church and the Presbyterian Church merged, and the following year, as the United Reformed Church, issued an invitation to the English Churches to enter into preliminary discussions with the intention that negotiations for union should begin quickly between those Churches which saw this step as practicable. All the major Churches, including the Roman Catholic Church, accepted the invitation to preliminary discussion. Even if later any Church feels that union at this time is not practicable it can remain associated with the further discussion.

The Church of England is also in consultation with the Roman Catholic Church and the Orthodox Churches and real developments in mutual understanding and acceptance have taken place. A Roman Catholic-Anglican Joint Commission has agreed statements on the Eucharist and the Ministry.

Besides discussion between the Churches, actual co-operation with the Protestant Churches and Roman Church is growing, not only in social affairs but also in the whole Church's ministry to the nation. Where there is particularly close co-operation in a locality churches may share buildings or establish a joint organisation.

The British Council of Churches, of which the Church of England has been a member from the beginning, came into being in 1942 as a fellowship of Churches ' which confess the Lord Jesus Christ as God and Saviour according to the Scriptures and therefore seek to fulfil together their common calling to the glory of the one God, Father, Son and Holy Spirit.' The Churches work together and there is a small secretariat to assist in carrying out work for all the Churches. Another organisation of the British Churches is the Churches Main Committee which was started to negotiate with the Government over war damage and has continued in being for negotiation over legislation generally.

Since 1910 there have been meetings of representatives of Churches from various parts of the world and in 1948 the World Council of Churches came into being. Assemblies are held about every seven years. Between Assemblies responsibility for the work of the WCC is carried by a Central Committee and other committees in which members of the Church of England participate. It has a secretariat in Geneva.

In 1964 a Conference of European Churches was set up. Churches from most countries in Eastern and Western Europe participate. The closer links of this country with Europe will clearly affect relationships with the Churches there. At present the Anglican diocese of Gibraltar covers Southern Europe and parts of the Mediterranean coast of Asia and Africa, while Northern Europe is under the jurisdiction of the Bishop of London for whom the Bishop of Fulham acts. The chaplaincies are not part of the Church of England. The American Church also has chaplaincies there under the care of an American bishop. The establishment of a diocese for Europe is under discussion.

Further afield the Church of England contributes to the life of other Anglican Churches through the missionary societies, of which the largest are the Church Missionary Society and the United Society for the Propagation of the Gospel.

THE ESTABLISHMENT

The brief historical sketch in the last chapter showed how the State and the Church grew together in close involvement. This involvement remains. The Church is not outside society, it is within it permeating it, or should be. It is sometimes necessary for the Church to judge or exhort the community, but this judgement or exhortation is given in the context of a close relationship not from outside.

The Queen ' acting according to the laws of the realm is the highest power under God in this Kingdom, and has supreme authority over all persons in all causes, as well ecclesiastical as civil '. The Queen is herself part of the Church and is crowned and anointed by the Church.

There are a number of expressions of the establishment. Public worship has been controlled by Parliament, though this control was eased in 1965 and if Parliament agrees will largely disappear with the passing of the Church of England (Worship and Doctrine) Measure. Diocesan bishops are appointed by the Crown on the advice of the Prime Minister, and the majority of them sit in the House of Lords, as leaders of the State as well as of the Church. The Synod legislates by Measure and Canon and these are recognised as part of the law. Ecclesiastical courts are courts of the land, not merely private tribunals.

For the purpose of this book the most important expression of the establishment is the special relationship between the parish clergy and their parishioners. Indeed it is probably right to say that this really is the most important expression, though it does not arouse discussion and controversy to the same extent as other aspects of the subject.

In 1970 the Church and State Commission reported. Thirteen of the sixteen members who signed the report were in favour of the continuance of the establishment with modifications and three preferred disestablishment. It is always possible that the developing situation will make disestablishment the appropriate answer but at present there seems no strong demand for it either inside or outside the Church. Reference has been made to the Church of England (Worship and Doctrine) Measure which is the result of the Commission's recommendations on worship and doctrine. There will be further references to these and other proposals of the Commission.

THE CHURCH AND THE LAW

All Churches and institutions in this country are subject to the law of the country. But for the Church of England owing to its special relationship with the State the law is unusually complex. The main sources of law are Acts of Parliament, Measures of the Church Assembly, Canons of the Convocations, Measures and Canons of the General Synod, rules and orders made under Acts, Measures or Canons, the Common Law and decisions of the Courts both secular and ecclesiastical. Measures are passed by the General Synod but require the consent of Parliament (who cannot amend them) before they receive the Royal Assent. Canons receive the Royal Assent without being laid before Parliament but they will not receive it if they contravene statute law. Various persons and bodies have authority under the law to make binding decisions, but these decisions are not strictly part of the law though they are enforceable.

The existence of this complex body of law can raise difficulties by impeding desirable reforms and by making the life of the Church unduly rigid. The tendency is to make the law more flexible and to lessen the area covered by law. This approach was strongly encouraged by the Church and State Commission.

The law can be enforced in the Courts, sometimes the secular courts, sometimes special ecclesiastical courts, which are recognised as part of the judicial system of the country. They used to have a wide jurisdiction over morals and over matrimonial and testamentary law, but now cases are virtually confined to those relating to alterations to church buildings and churchyards and the discipline of the clergy either on doctrinal or moral grounds or for a breach of some duty by action or neglect. The present system is set out in the Ecclesiastical Jurisdiction Measure 1963.

BISHOPS

Canon C.1 begins ' The Church of England holds and teaches that from the Apostles' time there have been three orders in Christ's Church: bishops, priests and deacons '.

The two senior bishops are the Archbishops of Canterbury and York. Each has jurisdiction over his province and each has his place in the Church of England as a whole. The Archbishop of Canterbury is the senior and is called Primate of All England and Metropolitan. The Archbishop of York is called Primate of England and Metropolitan.

There are 43 dioceses. Diocesan bishops owe allegiance to their archbishops. But subject to the law each diocese is very much a separate entity under its own diocesan. Within the diocese the clergy owe obedience to the bishop, but they have their position safeguarded by the law. Many clergymen have freehold offices from which at law they cannot be removed save in exceptional circumstances. It will be seen therefore that authority in the Church usually rests on respect and persuasion rather than compulsion.

The bishop is the chief pastor of the clergy and laity in his diocese and is responsible for the teaching of sound doctrine. He is to be an example of godly living and maintain quietness, love and peace among all men. The clergy act under his authority and assist him in his cure of souls over the diocese. He has rights over church buildings and the proper performances of church services. He celebrates or authorises other bishops to celebrate the rites of ordination and confirmation. He presides over his diocesan synod.

There are usually within a diocese one or more bishops suffragan, each of whom carries out duties assigned to him by his diocesan. There may be other bishops holding office or residing in the diocese, who assist the diocesan.

The question of how the bishops' various tasks can best be performed is now before the Synod in a report called ' Episcopacy in the Church of England ' by Canon P. A. Welsby which summarises work done over the past ten years. The diocesan bishop has the care of his diocese and also central duties on behalf of the Church and community. The full and proper performance of these tasks is beyond the powers of any individual. If there were many smaller dioceses the local task would be easier, but the central task would be more difficult, and the cost of administration would be high. Should there be some regional system for administration possibly by creating more provinces? Or should the present large dioceses remain, but the position of the suffragan bishops be strengthened in particular so that they could relieve the diocesan of local pastoral care of specific areas? Should dioceses follow local government boundaries? This is administratively convenient, but there are other pastoral factors. It would be convenient for local dialogue between the Churches if their boundaries were the same. So many questions can be asked and conflicting arguments arise. One important point is that a full-scale re-organisation of diocesan areas over the whole country would take up a large amount of time and thought and also money. There are however certain areas such as the great conurbations where re-organisation is particularly urgent. Small alterations of diocesan boundaries can be carried out now under the Pastoral Measure 1968.

Bishops receive authority by their consecration which is carried out by at least three bishops, one of whom is normally the archbishop of the province. Diocesan bishops are nominated by the Queen on the advice of the Prime Minister after a very full and careful inquiry as to opinion in the Church at large and in the diocese. Bishops suffragan are also nominated by the Queen but the person proposed by the diocesan is in practice chosen as a matter of course.

The whole question of the right way of appointing bishops was considered by the Commission on Church and State. The conclusion reached was that there should be an electoral body representing both the diocese and the church at large. The Commission was divided as to whether this body should give advice to the Crown through the Prime Minister or whether it should present the name of the person chosen directly to the Sovereign. Diocesan and suffragan bishops should be appointed in the same way, save that the consent of the diocesan should be required for the appointment of a suffragan. There have been two debates in the Synod and a conclusion will be necessary soon on which of these two proposals is preferable or whether there is a better third solution. Negotiations with the State authorities would then be necessary. The Commission also propose that leading members of other Churches should be invited to sit in the House of Lords as well as bishops of the Church of England.

CLERGY

Clergy are ordained as deacons and, usually a year later, are then ordained as priests. A central body known as the Advisory Council for the Church's Ministry (ACCM), which will be mentioned again later, normally acts on behalf of the bishops in advising whether men are suitable. Training takes place in theological colleges which are private institutions, but subject to a measure of Church control, partly because a large part of the college fees is paid from the General Synod's funds. Partly owing to the decline in the number of ordination candidates, but also for the provision of better and less expensive training, some colleges are combining or closing down.

The diocesan bishop or another bishop acting on his behalf ordains the man and it is his responsibility that the man is suitable from the point of view of doctrinal views, character and health. A deacon must ordinarily be 23 years of age and a priest 24. Unless a person holds an educational post or is a member of a religious community a clergyman must be ordained to a title, that is some Church office, usually a curacy. There are strict rules limiting the work a clergyman may do while officiating as such. Therefore the Church takes responsibility for him. But the primary responsibility for finding work rests with the man himself and he is free to take up a post which is offered to him. He can resign the exercise of his orders and be treated at law as if he were a layman, but he remains an ordained person. He can also be deprived of his right to exercise his orders, and also deposed from his orders if found guilty of serious misconduct by an ecclesiastical or civil court.

Usually a clergyman exercises his ministry in a parish and parochial clergymen are considered in the next chapter. But there are also a growing number of other posts, such as chaplaincies to institutions including hospitals, prisons, schools, universities, or special ministries to youth, industry and so on. In the complexity of modern life the co-operation between parochial and special ministries is increasingly important. Those exercising special ministries generally do so under a licence from the bishop and are responsible directly to him.

The general position of the clergy has been under investigation by the Church for some years in connection with various reports such as the *Paul Report, Partners in Ministry* and reports of the Terms of Ministry Committee. References will be made to particular questions in later passages.

LAITY

Bishops, clergy and laity are all equally members of the Church and each has his particular part to play. Lay people may hold special offices in the Church or be members of synods, committees and other bodies. Usually however they play their part in Church life in their parishes and in the places where they live and work.

It is impossible to define precisely who are members of the Church of England. Any baptised person who is an Englishman or resident in England can claim membership of the Church of England. Confirmation is not a requirement of membership but only confirmed persons can take part in the full life of the Church and certain offices can only be held by practising communicants. If formal reception into the Church is desired it should be by baptism or confirmation or a special form approved by the Convocations, as appropriate.

A lay person has certain rights and privileges in the parish in which he resides or in which he attends worship.

THE GENERAL SYNOD

The General Synod is the central legislative and deliberative body of the Church. It succeeded to all the powers of the Church Assembly and most of those of the Convocations. It can make decisions on behalf of the whole Church and those decisions may relate to doctrine, services and relations with other Churches. It can pass Measures which if accepted by Parliament have the force of Acts of Parliament on receipt of the Royal Assent. The Convocations remain in being as bodies which represent the two Provinces of Canterbury and York and as bodies able to speak particularly for the clergy, though there is power for a lay house of the province to sit with either Convocation if desired. In practice they meet rarely for limited purposes.

There are three houses in the General Synod. The House of Bishops consists of the Upper Houses of the two Convocations, that is the 43 diocesan bishops, but from the next election in 1975 there will also be six suffragans in the Upper House of Canterbury and three in the Upper House of York elected by their fellow suffragans in the province. The House of Clergy consists of the Lower Houses of the two Convocations, a maximum of 262 members as opposed to the previous 351 members. There are 15 representatives of the deans and provosts, one archdeacon for each diocese, six university proctors, representatives of the religious communities, the Channel Islands and the chaplains to the forces, not more than 191 proctors elected by the clergy of the dioceses, up to five *ex officio* members and up to three co-opted members. The House of Laity has up to seven *ex officio* members, two representatives of the religious communities, up to five co-opted members and not more than 250 diocesan representatives elected by the lay members of the deanery synods. The maximum is 262 as opposed to the previous 347 members in the Assembly.

CENTRAL ADMINISTRATION

The Church has no single centre of authority, but there are in fact three main centres.

The Archbishops of Canterbury and York, as primates of the Church in this country, have their headquarters at Lambeth Palace and Bishopthorpe, York.

The General Synod ordinarily meets in Church House by Westminster Abbey. The building is the headquarters of its own office and of a number of other bodies which are largely financed by a central fund to which the dioceses contribute. The chief officer of the Synod is the Secretary-General, who must be a layman. He has a small legal and administrative staff and is responsible for co-ordinating the work of the staffs of the departments. The Standing Committee of the Synod advises it on general policy, oversees the whole Church House organisation and is responsible for the conduct of business through the Synod. The Central Board of Finance is the financial executive of the Synod and is in close relationship with diocesan boards of finance. ACCM is concerned with the recruitment, selection and training of ordination candidates, post-ordination training, and general policy with relation to the ministry ordained and lay. The Board of Education is concerned with the Church's place in the State system of education and with the special training of church people. The Board for Mission and Unity stimulates in the Church a conviction of responsibility for mission and unity and keeps in touch with other Churches and agencies of the Churches. The Board for Social Responsibility has wide terms of reference including moral and social welfare, liaison with the social services, industry and migration abroad. The Council for Places of Worship advises the Synod and assists those concerned on buildings for worship. The Church Information Office is responsible for publicity, and there are a few smaller bodies which also derive their authority from the General Synod.

The third centre is 1 Millbank, by the Houses of Parliament, the home of the Church Commissioners. In 1948 this body succeeded to the powers of the Ecclesiastical Commissioners and Queen Anne's Bounty. The Commissioners manage the historic capital endowments of the Church and must do so in accordance with the trusts imposed on them by law. They are the Central Stipends Authority for the Church with the duty of co-ordinating the payment of the clergy. They pay about three-quarters of the stipends of the clergy and pensions for clergy and their widows and dependents. They assist towards the improvement of housing for the clergy. They help to finance churches and other buildings in new housing areas and also church schools. The

Commissioners also have a number of administrative duties in particular in connection with pastoral reorganisation and the property of the clergy. The Church Commissioners consist of all the diocesan bishops, the three Church Estates Commissioners, five deans or provosts of cathedrals, ten clergymen and ten laymen appointed by the General Synod, four nominees of the Queen and four of the Archbishop of Canterbury. Certain high officers within the State and the community are *ex officio* members.

There are a number of other organisations at work in the centre, a few statutory but mostly voluntary. Important examples are the missionary societies.

The organisation of the Church at the centre is complex and thought is being given either to simplification or improved co-operation. Simplification has obvious advantages, but organisations have grown up to meet needs and it could happen that a streamlined organisation failed to meet the needs or to arouse the support in service and money that is now willingly given, particularly if there was any question of proposing the merging of bodies that are now voluntary and independent.

THE DIOCESAN SYNOD

The diocesan synod succeeded to the powers of the diocesan conference. It is smaller and it should therefore be easier for it to work effectively. This means, however, that there cannot be direct parochial representation as there used to be in most dioceses. The deaneries are however strengthened, so that they form a real link between the parish and the diocese.

The synod considers and makes provision for matters affecting the Church in the diocese, and can express its mind on matters of religious and public interest, but may not purport to define doctrine. The bishop consults it on matters of general concern and importance to the diocese. It considers matters referred to it by the General Synod. Important questions are referred to diocesan synods, and no permanent changes can be made to the services of Baptism or Holy Communion or the Ordinal nor can there be a substantial change in relationship with another Church without the approval of the majority of diocesan synods. A

22

Measure is expected to be in operation shortly which makes such approval unnecessary in the case of overseas Churches. There must be a two-way traffic of consultation between the synod and the deanery synods and parishes, and opportunity must be given to them to raise questions at meetings of the synod.

There are three authorities in the diocesan synod, the bishop, the house of clergy and the house of laity. The total membership must be between 150 and 270 (or 500 in the case of London Diocese). The house of clergy includes the suffragan and assistant bishops, the dean or provost, the archdeacons and members elected by the houses of clergy of the deanery synods. The house of laity includes members elected by the houses of laity of the deanery synods. The members of the General Synod representing the diocese, the chancellor and the chairman of the board of finance are *ex officio* members, and each house can co-opt up to five members. The bishop may nominate up to ten members.

The synod can put forward to the General Synod a scheme revising its own composition. No synod has in fact yet done so.

DIOCESAN ADMINISTRATION

The bishop's council and standing committee of the synod is the general policy body of the diocese and can act for the synod when it is not meeting. Its membership is laid down in the Standing Orders of the diocesan synod. The diocesan board of finance holds property and acts as the financial executive of the diocese and levies quotas on the parishes. In some dioceses the work is divided between a board of finance and a diocesan trust. The bishop must be a member of the board and at least three-quarters of the members must be elected by the diocesan synod or deanery synods and a majority must be laymen.

There is a pastoral committee for pastoral reorganisation, a parsonages board for parsonage house matters, and an education committee for the educational work of the diocese with a particular concern for church schools. Various other committees are required by law and a diocesan synod can set up other committees for such Church purposes as it chooses, for example, mission, ecumenical work and social responsibility.

The diocese has its legal officers, the chancellor, who acts as judge on behalf of the bishop in faculty and discipline cases, and the registrar and legal secretary who advises the bishop and keeps the necessary records. Sometimes the registrar and legal secretary are different persons. The General Synod has approved proposals for the reorganisation of the duties and conditions of service of legal officers, in particular to remove unnecessary complexities which waste time and money.

CATHEDRALS

The principal church of the diocese is the cathedral. Though it is the church where the bishop has his throne and certain rights of use of the building, his general authority over it is rather less than over a parish church. He is the 'visitor', but only to a limited extent or not at all the 'ordinary' with jurisdiction over it.

The ancient cathedrals are governed by an administrative chapter consisting of the dean and the residentiary canons. There is a wider general chapter which also includes the honorary canons, but this has little authority. Most such cathedrals have no parish, only a close. Cathedrals of modern dioceses often have parishes. They are governed either by an administrative chapter or more often by a cathedral council consisting of clergy and laity. The principal clergyman who is also incumbent of the parish is called the provost, except in St Albans, where there is a dean.

A report made to the Church Assembly in 1969 by the Cathedrals and New Dioceses Committee suggested that the law should permit a more flexible approach. Besides the existing systems there should be the possibility of using a parish church with less elaborate organisation or having a centre of Christian community which provided not only a place of worship but conference and reading rooms and possibly residential accommodation. A diocese should not have to have a cathedral at all, but if so there would be a need for a central diocesan staff to fulfil the diocesan functions normally carried out by the cathedral staff. A diocese might find it convenient to have two or more diocesan churches rather than one. The Synod has not had time to consider this report, but cathedral organisation will require further thought when this is practicable.

The deans and some residentiary canons are appointed by the Queen on the advice of the Prime Minister, and most provosts, most other residentiary canons and honorary canons are appointed by the bishop. They almost invariably have freehold appointments. Minor canons and lay officers are usually appointed by the administrative chapter or council. The conditions of service of cathedral clergy will need working out in the light of any changes made in the method of appointing bishops and in the law relating to the clergy generally.

ARCHDEACONRIES AND DEANERIES

Most dioceses are divided into two or three archdeaconries each with its archdeacon appointed by the bishop. An archdeacon may also be a bishop suffragan which is particularly appropriate if a suffragan has the area of the archdeaconry under his special care. He assists the bishop in his pastoral care and 'visits' parishes annually except when the bishop is ' visiting '. He has special care for the clergy and while his name is to some extent associated with discipline his real concern is for their well-being and their effective ministry to their laity. He has a duty to see that church buildings are kept in proper order. He used to hold a court for trying the more trivial ecclesiastical cases, but such jurisdiction became obsolete and is now abolished. The archdeaconry does not have its own synod. There is a case for this where it is also an episcopal area.

An archdeaconry is divided into deaneries each with its rural dean. He presides over the deanery chapter and is joint chairman of the deanery synod which is described below. He is close enough to the clergy to know them well and can keep the bishop informed of anything that he need know. He has particular responsibilities if a parish has no incumbent. The rural dean is usually appointed by the bishop but in some dioceses there are special arrangements for his appointment or election.

One of the most important objects of the Synodical Government Measure was to strengthen Church organisation at the deanery level. Under the previous law it was not even necessary to have ruridecanal conferences. The deanery synods that replaced them must be established in every deanery and careful provision is made for them. The parish may be too small a unit for effective and imaginative local action, while the diocese may seem remote. If the deanery synod has a flourishing life there can be an important new element in the witness of the Church. How far this has been achieved naturally varies from one deanery to another. Because of the special place of the deanery synod and its close relationship with the parishes a fuller account is given of it.

The task of the deanery synod is set out in section 5 of the Synodical Government Measure:—

It considers matters concerning the Church of England and makes provision for such matters in relation to the deanery, and considers and expresses opinion on any other matters of religious or public interest.

It brings together the views of the parishes of the deanery on common problems, discusses and formulates common policies on those problems, fosters a sense of community and interdependence among the parishes, and generally promotes in the deanery the whole mission of the Church, pastoral, evangelistic, social and ecumenical.

It makes known and so far as appropriate puts into effect any provision made by the diocesan synod.

It considers the business of the diocesan synod, and particularly any matters referred to it by the General Synod, and sounds parochial opinion whenever this is required or appropriate.

It raises such matters as it considers appropriate with the diocesan synod.

The deanery synod thus has important duties in its own right and is the connecting link between the diocese and the parishes. Its house of laity is now the electoral body for members of the House of Laity of the General Synod.

The diocesan synod can give tasks to the deanery synods, including settling the parishes' shares in the quota. It is not the function of the synod to purport to define doctrine.

In the deanery synod there is a house of clergy consisting of all rectors, vicars and curates in the parishes, chaplains of institutions in the deanery, clerical members of the General Synod and diocesan synod resident in the deanery, and such other clergymen holding the bishop's licence and resident or working in the deanery as the diocesan synod may decide.

There is also a house of laity consisting of the parochial representatives elected at annual meetings, any lay member of the General or diocesan synod whose name is on a roll in the deanery, and such deaconesses or whole-time lay workers licensed to work in the deanery as the deanery synod may resolve. The new revision of the Church Representation Rules allows a bishop to add a lay representative of any non-parochial community in the deanery served by a chaplain. This addition is important in that it recognises that local church life is not only parochial, but that laity as well as clergy may properly participate in church life through their occupations rather than through their parishes.

Either house can co-opt members who are clergymen or communicant members of the laity as the case may be. The number of co-opted members must not exceed five per cent of the total membership.

The rural dean and a lay member elected by the house of laity are joint chairmen.

Parochial representatives of the laity hold offlce for three years beginning on 1st June after their election. The diocesan synod decides how many representatives each parish shall have, and the numbers must be related to the numbers on the electoral rolls of the parishes though not necessarily in a strict proportion.

The maximum number of members of the synod is 150 unless there are more than 75 clergymen in which case the lay members may be made equal. While it is not contemplated that the clergy should outnumber the laity there is no requirement for equality between the two Houses. The minimum number is 50 unless a synod of this size is impracticable.

This organisation can be varied by scheme made by the diocesan synod and laid before the General Synod.

The constitution of the deanery synod as described here is set out in Rules 19–21 of the Church Representation Rules which are a schedule to the Synodical Government Measure.

3.   The Parish

Nearly the whole of England is covered by parishes.   There are a few places not within parishes such as the closes of ancient cathedrals and some areas occupied by the army or air force. Parishes seem to have been gradually created between the seventh and thirteenth centuries and the boundary was often that of the manor.   They were areas of civil as well as ecclesiastical administration and often still are.

Before the coming into operation of the Pastoral Measure 1968 a parish had to have a suitable parish church.   Until one was built the area was called an ecclesiastical district.   Now provided there is proper provision for worship a parish church is no longer necessary and ecclesiastical districts have all become parishes. There is however occasionally a conventional district, that is an area taken from one or more parishes and administered on an experimental basis as a separate unit.   This arrangement is made by an agreement between the bishop and the incumbent or incumbents concerned.   Unless the experiment fails the district is expected to become a parish in due time.   It is under the care of a curate in charge.   For most practical purposes of ordinary day to day Church life the conventional district can be regarded as a parish and the curate in charge as an incumbent.

THE BENEFICE

A parish is under the care of an incumbent, who has ' the cure of souls '.   His cure is part of the wider cure of the bishop over the whole diocese. The office of the incumbent is called his benefice.   The area of the benefice is usually a single parish but can be more than one.   A clergyman can also hold two or more adjoining benefices ' in plurality '.   Parishes under the care of one clergyman are separate entities as far as parish organisations are concerned.

Except where there is a vacancy almost every place and every person resident in it are under the care of a clergyman.   Particularly in large towns it is impossible for a clergyman to know all his people, but at least he is there available to them if they wish to come to him. It is his right to visit them if he is able. They can claim his care and attention when they need it. This special relationship with the people of this country belongs to the Church of England clergy only. Obviously discretion is needed particularly towards those belonging to other Churches or unbelievers.

Traditionally the parish boundary was regarded as of great importance and if a clergyman ministered to people in his neighbour's parish he committed an offence. Today the system is much less rigid. In city areas particularly parish boundaries are largely meaningless and those who attend worship go to the church of their choice. But it is still necessary to keep the parochial system for determining rights of marriage and burial, for the sake of the ministry to those who do not go to church, for visiting and for undertakings such as Christian Aid Week collecting

Since the last century institutions with chapels could be placed under the care of the chaplain and removed from that of the incumbent of the parish. This can now happen where there is a chaplain whether or not there is a chapel. A clergyman can now minister outside his parish to persons on the church electoral roll of his parish and their households. In other cases, strictly, he requires the consent of the incumbent. Rules of this kind have to be interpreted with common sense, especially in the case of ministers who are licensed by the bishop to a special assignment other than an institution.

TEAMS AND GROUPS

The Pastoral Measure 1968 permits more complex forms of parochial organisation called teams and groups. Before the passing of this Measure parochial clergymen were either incumbents, each in charge of his own completely separate area, or assistant curates each clearly subordinate to an incumbent. The law did not visualise the possibility of a partnership of more or less equal people.

In a team ministry the area of a benefice, which may include one or more parishes, is placed under the care not of an individual incumbent but of a team of clergymen. There is a leader called the rector, and his colleagues who are called vicars are to be regarded as of the same status as a vicar with his own benefice and parish. The rector holds the benefice but the vicars share his cure of souls. A vicar could have the cure of a special area which might be a parish, or he could have a special task over the whole area such as youth or industrial work, or he could hold a chaplaincy in an institution, or he could share generally in the rector's cure. The rector and vicars meet periodically as a chapter. There could also be assistant curates or lay workers, but they would not be members of the team, though they could be invited to be present at chapter meetings.

In a group ministry a number of incumbents work together as a group. Each has authority in his own parish but the others in the group help him where appropriate, just as he helps them under their authority in their parishes. The incumbents meet periodically as a chapter and provision must be made for a chairman. There could also be a group council of clergy and laity, but authority would still rest with the parochial church councils of the parishes.

Ministers of other Churches cannot legally be included in a team or group but by invitation they can participate fully in the work, and can attend chapter meetings provided they do not have their votes recorded in the not very likely event of votes being taken.

INCUMBENTS

The general position of the incumbent has been described. He has the cure of souls of the parish and a general responsibility as the representative of the Church in the parish. He is the leader, but as always leadership may have a rather different meaning in the Church to that normally accepted in the community. He has certain rights of decision particularly over the services of the Church, but if the Church of England (Worship and Doctrine) Measure comes into operation the choice of the forms of service to be used will be a matter of joint decision between the incumbent and the parochial church council. He has authority over his curates and lay workers. He is chairman of the parochial church council but cannot control its exercise of its powers. His authority depends upon his personality and persuasiveness and upon their sense of respect and goodwill.

An incumbent is either a rector or a vicar. The original distinction between the two was that the rector acted in his own right and received all the profits of the benefice. The vicar was the deputy for the rector, who might be another clergyman or a religious house, or a college or a layman. The rector and vicar would divide the profits of the benefice. There is now no real practical distinction between the two kinds of incumbent except in teams.

Incumbents are chosen by patrons. The patron is often the bishop but may be the Crown, a chapter or college or other institution, or a trust, or another incumbent or a lay person. Each diocese has a patronage board but usually these do not present to many benefices. Sometimes the parishioners are the patron. There are special rather complicated rules about the appointment of rectors in team ministries. Vicars in team ministries are appointed by the bishop and the rector jointly.

The bishop must institute a clergyman presented to him by a patron unless he has a very strong reason to the contrary. The parochial church council can now have a say in the appointment. Chapter 14 describes the process of admitting an incumbent to office.

The patronage system grew up in the past and is in principle hardly in accord with general present day thinking. It has certain practical advantages together with some disadvantages. The existence of patrons with rights of patronage in various parts of the country tends to facilitate the movement of clergy between dioceses. The parties obviously involved in an appointment are the diocesan authorities, the parishioners and the clergyman himself. It is not in fact very easy to work out a satisfactory system which keeps the interests of all concerned in proper balance. This whole problem has been under consideration by the Church for some time in connection with the report *Partners in Ministry,* and subsequent reports of the Terms of Ministry Committee. No solution has commended itself to the General Synod, but there seems to be a clear view that the present system is unsatisfactory.

There used to be a considerable traffic in rights of patronage either for the purpose of imposing a doctrinal viewpoint on a parish or for financial and family reasons. In general now rights of patronage may not be sold and there is a careful procedure for voluntary transfer. The churchwardens and secretary of the parochial church council are informed and objections can be made to the bishop, who communicates them to the patron. The patron can however disregard the objections.

The incumbent holds his benefice as a freehold. That means he cannot be deprived of it except for incapacity through ill health or following upon a court order involving serious misconduct. A Measure has just been introduced, which would permit the removal of an incumbent for pastoral reasons with suitable safeguards.

There is at present no retiring age, but a Measure has been introduced which would require retirement from freehold offices including bishoprics, archdeaconries and cathedral offices as well as benefices at seventy or shortly afterwards. A clergyman could continue to exercise his ministry in other offices without having a freehold. The Measure is not intended to apply to holders of existing offices so long as they remain in them.

A benefice can be dissolved through pastoral reorganisation and in that case the incumbent must be given another acceptable office or be compensated. A rector in a team ministry may have a freehold or hold his benefice for a term of years. Vicars in team ministries always hold office for a term of years.

Most benefices have stipends attached to them. These are paid either out of the Church Commissioners funds or from profits from land owned by the incumbent, which is called glebe, or from trust funds, or a combination of these. In fact the stipend is rarely adequate and has to be made up to a suitable sum by the diocese or parish. There is usually a parsonage house in which the incumbent is expected to live, though for good reason he may be allowed to live elsewhere in the parish or even outside it.

Pensions are normally payable to all clergymen whether incumbents or not at the age of 68 or there can be early retirement at 65 or because of disability.

The question of the payment and housing of the clergy is considered more fully in Chapter 13. The particular duties of incumbents and others are discussed in later chapters as appropriate.

ASSISTANT CURATES

Assistant curates are licensed by the bishop on the nomination of the incumbent, who has to ensure that the curate is paid a proper stipend and has somewhere to live. Almost invariably the parochial church council is involved in these matters.

The curate does his work under the authority of the incumbent. Sometimes he is given the care of a particular church building or area or a particular special function in the parish. Otherwise he works as directed by the incumbent.

A curate is subject to six months' notice. Usually the permission of the bishop is necessary before notice can be given. The bishop may revoke a curate's licence at any time for sufficient cause, but the curate has a right of appeal to the archbishop.

DEACONESSES AND WOMEN WORKERS

Women are admitted to the order of deaconesses by prayer and the laying on of hands by the bishop. Deaconesses are not in holy orders, as clergymen are. The bishop must ensure that they are fit persons in training, character and health.

A deaconess can be licensed to a parish by the bishop, who must ensure that adequate provision is made for her salary, insurance against sickness and pension. She assists the incumbent in pastoral care and by taking part in services.

A woman worker is in much the same position as a deaconess but she is commissioned for her work without laying on of hands. She is licensed under the same conditions as a deaconess. Her duties are not specified in the Canon but are usually pastoral.

For detailed provisions about deaconesses reference should be made to Section D of the Canons and about women workers to Canon E.7. Chapters 10 and 11 describe their special duties.

READERS

The other persons who are specially concerned with the pastoral side of the life of the parish and the taking of services are the readers. They may be men or women and must be baptised, confirmed and regular communicants. If a reader is to work in a parish he is to be nominated to the bishop by the incumbent. If he is to work in a wider area he is nominated by the archdeacon or rural dean after consulting the incumbent of his parish. The bishop must be satisfied that he is of good life, sound in faith and suitable to the work. The bishop or others acting on his behalf must examine him to assure themselves that he possesses a sufficient knowledge of holy Scripture and of the doctrine and worship of the Church of England and that he is able to read services properly and teach and preach. He must make and sign a declaration and is then admitted to office by the delivery to him of the New Testament, but without imposition of hands. He is then given a certificate of admission which is sufficient for any diocese in the Church of England.

In order to carry out his work a reader requires a licence or a written permission from the bishop. If a reader is to be a stipendiary reader (which is very unusual) the bishop must be satisfied about his stipend, insurance and pension. The bishop may cancel a reader's licence at any time if he thinks fit.

Detailed provisions about readers are contained in Canons E4, E5 and E6.

CHURCHWARDENS

The lay offices so far described are of recent prominence and relate to the conduct of services and pastoral care. The traditional lay leadership in the parish rests with the churchwardens, and because their office developed at a time when the differentiation between the work of clergy and laity was more pronounced than it is now there is a tendency to regard their concerns as financial and administrative. In fact they also have responsibilities for the worship and pastoral care of the parish.

The general task of the churchwarden is set out in paragraph 4 of Canon E.1:—

' The Churchwardens when admitted are officers of the Ordinary. They shall discharge such duties as are by law and custom assigned to them; they shall be foremost in representing the laity and in co-operating with the Incumbent; they shall use their best endeavours by example and precept to encourage the parishioners in the practice of true religion and to promote unity and peace among them. They shall also maintain order and decency in the church and churchyard especially during the time of Divine Service.'

There will be many references to the duties of churchwardens in relation to particular matters throughout this book. Their qualifications and method of appointment are set out in Chapter 6. Here it is sufficient to point out that they are not only parish officials, but are also officers of the ordinary, normally the bishop. They are in a personal relationship to him and to the wider Church.

SIDESMEN

The task of the sidesmen is set out in Canon E.2 and is 'to promote the cause of true religion in the parish and to assist the churchwardens in the discharge of their duties in maintaining order and decency in the church and churchyard, especially during the time of divine service'. They too have a general duty in the parish as well as their work in connection with church services. Their functions in past centuries, like those of the churchwardens, used to be wider, and extend to an oversight of the general spiritual and moral state of the people in the parish.

They are chosen at the annual meeting in the manner described in Chapter 5.

OTHER PARISH OFFICERS

The other ancient office is that of parish clerk. Only very few parishes still have them. Section 7 of the Parochial Church Councils (Powers) Measure 1956 provides that the appointment of parish clerks and sextons or anyone performing or assisting in the performance of their duties is a matter for the incumbent and the parochial church council jointly and that they jointly fix their terms of service.

Canon E.3 provides as follows:—

' In any parish in which the services of a parish clerk, sexton, verger, or other officer are required the minister and the parochial church council may in accordance with the law appoint some fit and proper person to these offices to perform such services upon such terms and conditions as they may think fit.'

The important parish officer who is not mentioned by name is the organist. His office is not recognised at law but depends on the contract of service of the individual organist. Forms of contract which are generally used are in existence. The legal point to note in connection with this office is that subject to the terms of any contract the use of the organ is controlled by the incumbent. Therefore it is necessary to make the position quite clear. If the incumbent unreasonably prevents the organist from playing he can appeal to the bishop to give suitable directions.

THE PAROCHIAL CHURCH COUNCIL

There have already been a number of references to the parochial church council and there will be many more to the duties of this body, which is or should be so important in the life of the parish. Its constitution and procedure are set out in Chapter 7.

The general duties of the parochial church council are contained in the Parochial Church Council (Powers) Measures, first of 1921 and then of 1956 which replaced it. Nearly the whole of these Measures were taken up with matters of property and administration, and there is the danger that the impression may be given that duties of this kind are the primary function of parochial church councils. This was never the intention. Section 2 of both Measures read: ' It shall be the primary duty of the council in every parish to co-operate with the minister in the initiation, conduct and development of church work both within the parish and outside it.' These wide functions are also emphasised later in section 7 of the 1956 Measure, where the council is given power to make representations to the bishop about any matter affecting the welfare of the Church in the parish.

When the Synodical Government Measure had been prepared and was being revised by the Assembly, the question was asked whether these general functions were a sufficient expression of synodical government in the parish. Section 6 of the Synodical Government Measure substituted a new section 2 in the 1956

Measure and gives the council wider and more clearly defined powers.

The incumbent and the parochial church council have the duty of consulting together on matters of general concern and importance to the parish. The council is also to co-operate with the incumbent in promoting in the parish the whole mission of the Church, pastoral, evangelistic, social and ecumenical. The incumbent and the council consult on matters of general concern and importance, including such matters as public worship. If the Church of England (Worship and Doctrine) Measure becomes law the incumbent and parochial church council will together decide what forms of services will be used in a parish. The incumbent's own pastoral care of individuals is not under the jurisdiction of the parochial church council.

The council can consider and discuss matters concerning the Church of England or any other matters of religious or public interest, but may not declare the doctrine of the Church on any question.

The council is the link between the parish and the diocesan and deanery synods. It makes known and puts into effect any provision made by the diocesan synod or the deanery synod, but without prejudice to the powers of the council on any particular matter. Where the council has its own clear responsibilities those outside can suggest but cannot dictate. It gives advice to the diocesan synod and the deanery synod on any matter referred to it. It raises such matters as it considers appropriate with the diocesan synod or deanery synod. So there is a two-way traffic.

In the exercise of its functions the council must take into consideration any expression of opinion by any parochial church meeting. It is not however bound by such expressions of opinion.

As has already been said in the historical introduction the parochial church council takes over most of the duties relating to property, finance and administration of the churchwardens and the vestry. Property and finance are considered in Chapter 8, and other special duties in various parts of this book.

THE PARISHIONERS AND THE CONGREGATION
The Church of England unlike other English Churches has both parishioners and congregations.

The parishioners are those who reside within the area of the parish and who have a right to receive the ministrations of the parish clergy. In particular, provided they carry out the proper rules and formalities, they have a right to baptism, marriage and a burial service in the parish church. They are the recipients of service offered by the Church if they choose to use them. For some of these services (but not baptism) they are liable to fees, but they have no longer any general obligations at law towards the Church.

The congregation are the practising laity of the Church. They may live in or outside the parish, but if they are non-resident they obtain the status of parishioners by having their names entered on the roll of the parish. Most offices in the Church require some kind of qualification of Church attendance, though entry on the roll for a resident in the parish does not.

Of course there is no clear line of demarcation between the parishioner and the member of the congregation. There is the person who turns up perhaps at the harvest festival or on Christmas Eve. There is the person who has his name entered on the roll just to oblige and does nothing about it.

There are always two lines of thinking, both of which are found in the Gospels. One can say that God requires of his people full service and nothing else is sufficient. One can say that God cares for all of us and that even the smallest service is acceptable to him. The Church of England firmly says both.

CO-OPERATION WITH OTHER CHURCHES

During the twentieth century there has been a tremendous growth in friendship and co-operation with other churches. However, this change is scarcely reflected in church law at all. Therefore co-operation proceeds outside the law, sometimes even in technical breach of it. When Canon Law was being revised in the 1950s and 1960s canons were prepared to authorise co-operation over church services. These were dropped because it was felt that the situation was too fluid. Thought is beginning to be given again to legal provision in this field.

Often clergymen and congregations of Churches worship and work closely together without any question of a common organisation arising. It may happen however that they wish to share the same building, either an existing one or a new one to be built. Legal provision was made for this situation by the Sharing of Church Buildings Act 1969, which is discussed in Chapter 16.

Sometimes, whether or not there is a shared building all the Churches in a place, or some of them, wish to share as far as possible a common life and a common organisation. This may happen in any kind of area, but it is particularly likely in a new housing area where there are no traditions. In recent years it has been officially recognised by the Churches that places may be designated Areas of Ecumenical Experiment. ' These are defined areas where, under responsible authority, certain denominational traditions are suspended for a period in order that the new patterns of worship, mission and ministry can be undertaken.' It is the usual practice to appoint a sponsoring body of representatives of the various Churches to watch over the experiment and provide guidance and control as appropriate.

In 1973 the Churches set up a ' Consultative Committee for Local Ecumenical Projects in England ' to assist and advise both those engaged in local projects and those sponsoring them. It is directly responsible to the member churches and formally independent of the British Council of Churches though it is in close relationship with it.

Areas of Ecumenical Experiment are therefore a new feature in the life of the Church but have no legal authority. From the point of view of the Church of England each such area is a parish or a group of parishes and in strict law should be organised as such. For the objects to be achieved the law may be ignored or lip service only be paid to it, while the reality is in the extra-legal life. The number of these areas is increasing, and it will probably soon be desirable to clarify their position, so that they are legally recognised without undue restrictions being laid upon them.

PART II—MACHINERY

The machinery of parish government is set out for the most part in the Church Representation Rules which are a schedule to the Synodical Government Measure. The references in brackets are to these Rules. The machinery for the choice of churchwardens set out in Chapter 8 is contained partly in the Rules and partly in the Churchwardens (Appointment and Resignation) Measure 1964.

Experience in the first few years has shown that there are certain features of the system that need improvement. Therefore the Church Representation Rules have been amended and these amendments came into operation on 1st January 1974. Those who use the Rules should obtain the new version (price 40p from the Church House Bookshop) as the previous one could be misleading.

This section contains procedure in which the laity are involved. Therefore it is very detailed. It is intended primarily for reference and is certainly not light reading.

4. The Church Electoral Roll

The Church's system of lay representation is a democratic system. The easiest method of approach is to begin from the electorate. Every parish must have a church electoral roll on which qualified persons may have their names entered. The rules as amended always refer to the ' church electoral roll ' or ' the roll ', as the term ' electoral roll ' can be confused in people's minds with the local government register of electors.

QUALIFICATIONS
Who should form the electorate was one of the most important questions that the Church had to decide in framing its system of representation in 1919. There were three possible lines that

might have been taken. It might have been said that the Church is the Established Church of the country and therefore anyone in the country ought to be permitted to vote; or that only members of the Church should be permitted to vote and that therefore the qualification should be baptism; or that the right should depend on participation in the life of the Church and therefore confirmation or communicant status or some qualification of church attendance should be required. In fact the Church decided on the middle course and those applying for enrolment had to be baptised and declare that they were members of the Church of England and did not belong to any religious body which was not in communion with the Church of England. In spite of subsequent questioning and hesitation the sufficiency of baptism as a qualification for enrolment has been maintained.

One aspect of the rules that was very carefully considered in the 1972–73 revision was the possibility of members of other Churches having their names entered on the parish rolls of the Church of England. Before the 1920s membership of the Church of England was not a necessary qualification for attending the vestry meeting. Such membership has however always been required for entry on the roll and attending the annual meeting. The 1969 solution was to require an applicant to state, first that he was a member of the Church of England or of another Church of the Anglican Communion or of an overseas Church in communion with the Church of England, and secondly that he was not a member of any other religious body which was not in communion with the Church of England.

Taking the first requirement, it seemed to be clearly right that a member of another Anglican Church who lives for a period in England should keep his allegiance to his own Church yet participate fully in the life of the Church of England. The same permission was extended to members of other overseas Churches in communion with the Church of England as their members living in England might be expected to want to share the life of our Church. There are not many such churches. The most important ones are united Churches in which the Anglicans have participated, such as the Churches of South India, North India and Pakistan. There are a few other Churches which are in communion with the Church of England, the most important being the

Old Catholic Church, a European Church centred on Utrecht in Holland. The Church of England is not in communion with any Church which ordinarily operates in England, and it was then thought that even if it was, the members of such Churches should join in the government of their own Churches.

When the rules were reconsidered the fact that there were no such Churches in England was noted, and account was also taken of the failure of the negotiations with the Methodists. The present formula seemed to have unfriendly overtones and to be unnecessarily complicated. The provisions in the rules and the application form for entry in the roll were altered so that an applicant has to declare that he is a member of the Church of England or of a Church in communion with the Church of England. It is emphasised that this change makes no practical difference at the moment and will not do so until the Church of England enters into communion with a Church ordinarily operating in England. If there is any doubt as to whether an overseas Church or a Church in England is in communion with the Church of England, the question is decided by the Archbishops (R.44(4)).

A change of greater practical importance is the omission of the requirement that a person applying for entry on the roll must declare that ' he is not a member of any other religious body which is not in communion with the Church of England '. The line had always been taken that membership of another Church was really incompatible with membership of the Church of England, certainly if the two churches were not in communion with each other. But since 1969 the important decision has been taken that communicant members of other Churches should be accepted in their own right at Church of England altars. Was there a case for admitting them also to participate in the government of the Church if they so wished? The answer given to the question stated in those terms was that the time had not yet come. Applicants must declare that they are members of the Church of England or of Churches in communion with it and by right of such membership only may their names be entered on the roll.

But there is another question. Supposing a person is involved in the life of two Churches, one of which is the Church of England, can he not declare himself a member of the Church of England, yet not deny his allegiance to the other Church? The new version of the rule allows this to happen. Provided a person feels able to make the declaration required no question will be asked as to his involvement in the life of other Churches.

While the Church of England and most other Trinitarian Churches accept baptism in any Church as entry into the one Church of God, nevertheless denominational differences are real and a member of one Church would usually not feel able to declare himself a member of another. There are, however, exceptional circumstances, where this is desired, regardless of the rigid requirements of logic. Examples are where husband and wife belong to different Churches, where there is no church of a particular Church available and its member identifies himself with the life of a congregation of another Church, or most significant when there is an area of ecumenical experiment or of particularly close co-operation so that the choice of one Church rather than another seems unnecessary and inappropriate (R.1(2)).

Those electing must also be responsible, and it is required that they must be at least 17 years old. Before 1957 the age used to be 18 but was lowered to encourage young people to take an active share in the life of the Church (R.1 (2)).

Being one of the electorate is a parish matter. Each parish must have an electoral roll (R.1 (3)). Any qualified person can have his name on the roll of a parish in which he resides; or he can have his name on the roll of the parish where he has habitually attended public worship for six months. What ' habitually ' means depends on the circumstances, but it does not necessarily imply great frequency (R.3 (2)). There is no question of any period of time when the application is based on residence, but the residence must be of a regular and not merely of a casual nature (R.44 (5)).

Under the 1969 rules a person could have his name entered on the rolls of two parishes, but no more, if he was qualified for both. The consent of the two parochial church councils was required. A person may now be on the rolls of any number of parishes if he has the necessary qualifications and no consents are required. He may then attend the annual meetings and stand for election to the parochial church councils. If however he wishes to stand for election to the deanery or other any higher synod he must choose one parish only for having the necessary qualification of entry on a roll (R.1 (3)).

Finally, if a person wishes to have his name entered on the roll of a parish he must sign an application form. The form set out in the 1969 Rule was rather complicated. Because of the changes made in the qualifications for entry it has been possible to produce a much simpler form drawn up on rather different lines, which it is hoped will be found by parish authorities to be a real improvement. This form will be found in the Appendix on page 68.

WHAT IS A PARISH?

As a result of the simplification of the system by the Pastoral Measure described in Chapter 3 it is only necessary to say that for the purpose of these rules conventional districts are regarded as being exactly the same as parishes, and so have rolls, annual meetings and parochial church councils (R.44(1)). The Rules also make special provision for Guild Churches in the City of London which are treated in many ways as if they were parish churches (R.4A).

WHAT IS A 'MINISTER'?

Another term which is used in this chapter and elsewhere in this booklet is ' minister '. Usually it means the rector or vicar of the parish. Where there is a vacancy it means a curate or a neighbouring clergyman if he is licensed to the charge of the parish, but does not include an assistant curate unless he is so licensed. A curate in charge of a conventional district is a minister, and also a vicar in a ' team ministry '. Who he is has been described in Chapter 3 (R.44 (1)).

KEEPING THE ROLL

The parochial church council is responsible for the keeping of the roll, or, until such time as the parochial church council is constituted, the minister and churchwardens (R.1 (4)). Names must be added or removed from time to time to keep the roll up to date (except between the time when the roll is exhibited and the annual meeting—see page 46) (R.1 (6)). Every parochial church council must appoint a church electoral roll officer to act on its behalf and

44

under its directions (R.1 (5)). Where practicable the address as well as the name must be entered on the roll (R.1 (9)).

REMOVAL OF NAMES

In general a person's name may be removed when he ceases to have a required qualification but for no other reason. Thus if a resident in the parish ceases to go to church his name may not be removed solely on that ground as attendance is not a necessary qualification for a resident. A person's name may be removed if he has died, or been ordained, or signified in writing his desire that his name should be removed, or ceased to reside in the parish, unless he continues to attend public worship in the parish habitually (even though he has not attended for the six months that would otherwise be necessary) or, not being resident, has not attended public worship for six months unless prevented by illness or other sufficient cause, or was not qualified to have his name entered when it was entered (R.1 (7)). Becoming a member of another Church not in communion with the Church of England or having his name entered on the roll of another parish without complying with the requirements of the rules have now ceased to be grounds for removal as a result of changes in the qualifications for entry which have been described. A person whose name is removed may have it entered again if he subsequently becomes so entitled (R.1 (8)).

NOTICES

When a person applies for entry on the roll of a parish and, in so applying, asks that his name should be removed from the roll of another parish, the council of the first parish must inform the council of the second. Where a person's name is removed from a roll because he has moved to another parish the council must whenever possible notify the council of that other parish (R3. (1) and (2)).

LIFE OF ROLL

Under the pre-1969 law a roll when once prepared went on indefinitely. Every year it was revised and names were removed if the person so wished or was no longer qualified. Rolls could become unrealistically inflated. Residents with little real contact might be enrolled or might once have been active members of the congregation but have ceased to be so. Their names would remain on the roll unless of their volition or with encouragement they signified their wish to have them removed. This situation could not arise with non-residents as for them there was a qualification of attendance at public worship. Even now the parish authorities might prefer to give them the benefit of the doubt rather than take action or ask questions that might be embarrassing. Particularly with churches with large congregations in city areas keeping account of attendance at worship is virtually impossible.

Under the 1969 Rules existing rolls continued until 1972, but before the annual meeting in that year a new roll had to be prepared and fresh applications were required from those who had been previously enrolled if they wished to continue to be enrolled and were still qualified. There will be new rolls in 1978, 1984 and every sixth year thereafter. In the intervening years there must be the usual annual revision. (R.2 (4)—(7.))

ANNUAL REVISION

The annual revision is conducted by or under the direction of the council. The minister is responsible for seeing that the appropriate notice of the revision (see Appendix, page 69) is displayed at the principal door of all churches and buildings licensed for public worship and remains there for at least 14 days, and the revision cannot begin before this period is over. The revision must end not less than 15 or more than 28 days before the annual parochial church meeting (R.2 (1)). During the revision all entries and removals since the last revision are reviewed and any further entries and removals made (R.2 (2)). When the revision is completed a copy of the roll and a list of the names removed since the last revision must be exhibited at the door of the parish church for not less than 14 days before the annual meeting and no further names may be added or removed until after the annual meeting (R.2 (3)).

PREPARATION OF NEW ROLL

When a new roll is to be prepared at least two months before the annual meeting, the minister is responsible for seeing that the appropriate notice (see Appendix, page 70) is displayed at the principal door of all churches and buildings licensed for worship and remains there for at least 14 days. In future, at every service held on each of the two Sundays within the fourteen days after affixing the notice, or if there is no service on either of these Sundays on the first subsequent Sunday on which there is a service, the person conducting the service must inform the congregation of the preparation of the new roll. (R.2 (4)).

The council has a duty to take reasonable steps to inform persons whose names are on the old roll that the new roll is being prepared and of the need for re-enrolment. The displaying of the notice is not sufficient by itself, but there should be further communication either by public announcement or personal contact verbally or in writing. The rule is deliberately worded rather vaguely because circumstances differ so much. Where the number is small personal contact either by letter or by announcement in church on a Sunday with a letter to those not present might be the answer. A notice in the parish magazine with a letter to households which do not take it would seem sufficient. Notices outside the churches and in other public places and announcements at services might in some circumstances be a proper solution, but it must be remembered that attendance at worship is not a qualification for entry for residents. If some method other than personal communication is used, the roll should be studied to ensure that there is no one in particular danger of being missed. Invalids or those living in remote farms or cottages are obvious examples. But the council is only required to take reasonable steps. For example if a person is totally absent and cannot be contacted without undue labour and expense there would be no need to contact him. (R.2 (5)).

The preparation of the new roll begins after the notice is displayed. All wishing to be enrolled must apply in the usual way and possess the usual qualifications. The only exception is that if a non-resident was previously enrolled, but has been prevented from attending public worship because of illness or other sufficient cause, his name may be entered. The reason or reasons for failure to attend must be stated in the application form. Probably sufficient cause should be interpreted rather narrowly. It would obviously include absence, and might include attendance on a sick person. But something which hinders or discourages does not necessarily prevent. Each situation would need considering on its own merits. The new roll must be completed between 15 and 28 days before the annual meeting (R.2 (6)).

A copy of the new roll must be displayed for not less than 14 days before the annual meeting at the principal door of the parish church. When it is affixed it comes into operation and the old roll ceases to have effect. No name may be added to the new roll between completion and the close of the annual meeting (R.2 (7)).

APPEALS

If anyone objects to an enrolment or refusal to enrol or the removal of a name or refusal to remove a name he can appeal to the rural dean, or if there is no rural dean to the archdeacon, within 14 days of the act or refusal or, if the matter arises at the annual revision or preparation of a new roll, on the publication of the roll. Unless agreement is reached the matter is referred to an electoral commission established by the diocesan synod, which hears the case and must give parties a right to appear in person or through a legal or other representative. (R.36.)

INSPECTION OF ROLL

The roll must be available for inspection by bona fide inquirers at all times (R.1 (1)).

ALTERATION OF BOUNDARIES

If the boundaries of a parish are altered the council of the parish which loses the area is responsible for approaching those resident in it whose names are on the roll and asking them whether they wish to be enrolled in their new parish. If they answer ' yes ' the council of the new parish is informed and enters the names without the necessity for an application. The persons concerned have the option either of transferring, or remaining on their present roll if they are habitual worshippers, or having their names entered on the roll of any other parish where they habitually worship (R.2 (8)).

CERTIFICATION OF NUMBERS

In some years the numbers on the roll need to be certified to the secretaries of the diocesan and deanery synods. The parish will be notified when it is necessary. The purpose is to enable the appropriate number of seats to be allocated to the parish on the deanery synod, to the deanery on the diocesan synod, and to the diocese on the House of Laity of the General Synod.

The numbers are needed every third year in the year before elections to deanery and diocesan synods take place, that is in 1975, 1978 and so on. Returns are also needed in the year before an election to the House of Laity of the General Synod. These take place every five years beginning in 1970. Therefore returns should be required in 1974, 1979 and 1984. In the last year they will also be required for deanery and diocesan elections because the two cycles coincide (R.4 (1)).

The certificate required from the parish, which must be returned by 1st July, sets out the number on the roll. It is no longer necessary to state whether a person has his name on the roll of another parish, and indeed the council may well not have this information. The certificate must be signed by the chairman, vice-chairman, secretary or church electoral roll officer of the parish. A copy must be displayed at the principal door of every parish or building licensed for worship in the parish for at least fourteen days (R.4).

5. The Annual Meeting

How do those who have their names on the electoral roll exercise their rights? By attending the annual parochial church meeting or ' annual meeting ' as it is usually called. There they hear reports on Church subjects and can raise matters for discussion themselves and vote in the elections.

WHO MAY ATTEND?

All those on the roll have the right to attend and take part in the discussions (R.5 (2)). There is no reason why others—should not attend, but they do so by courtesy. It should be made clear to whom the invitation is given, to individuals, to the Press, to anyone on the roll, to any parishioner or to whoever chooses to come. They could also be allowed to speak by invitation, but on no account may they vote. The clergy of the parish have the right to attend and take part. These include besides the rector or vicar, the curates of the parish or of any other parish united with it under the same benefice, vicars who are part of a team ministry which includes the parish, and the rector or vicar (but not the other clergy) of any parish which is joined with the parish in a group. Clergymen resident in the parish who are not beneficed in or licensed to any other parish may also attend. No clergyman may nominate candidates or vote in the elections of representatives of the laity (R.5 (3)).

TIME AND PLACE

The meeting must be held every year not later than 30th April (R.5 (1)). It used to be not later than the first week after Easter week. A fixed date seemed more appropriate partly because the day of the annual meeting is part of the timetable for a number of elections. The place, date and time may be fixed by a previous annual meeting or by the parochial church council, which may vary a decision of a previous annual meeting, or if neither body has fixed them, by the minister (R.6 (2)). Unless the parochial church council decides otherwise the meeting must be held in the parish (R.6 (4)).

CONVENING THE MEETING

The minister is responsible for convening the meeting, but if there is a vacancy or if for any reason he cannot act, the vice-chairman of the parochial church council convenes it, or failing him, the secretary or some other person appointed by the parochial church council (R.6 (4)). He must see that the proper notice (see Appendix, page 71) is displayed at the principal door of all churches and buildings licensed for public worship in the parish for a period including the last two Sundays before the day of the meeting (R.6 (1)).

PROCEDURE

The minister, if present, is chairman, or failing him, the vice-chairman of the parochial church council, or failing him a person chosen by the meeting. The chairman may vote and also have a casting vote, except that a clerical chairman has no vote of any kind in the elections of representatives of the laity (R.7). The secretary of the parochial church council or some other person appointed by the meeting acts as clerk and takes the minutes (R.8 (8)). There is power to adjourn. Otherwise the meeting determines its own rules of procedure (R.8 (7)).

BUSINESS INITIATED BY THE PAROCHIAL CHURCH COUNCIL

The parochial church council presents for discussion at the meeting a copy or copies of the roll, an annual report on the proceedings of the council and on the financial affairs of the parish, the audited accounts of the council for the year ending on the preceding 31st December, an audited statement of the funds and property of the council at that date, and a report on the fabric, goods and ornaments of the church or churches of the parish. The council is also required to present a report on the proceedings of the deanery synod (R.8 (1)). This is provided by the deanery synod (R.23 (1) (f)). A copy of the audited accounts and of the audited statement of the council's funds and property must be displayed at the principal door of every church and building licensed for worship at least seven days before the meeting. They are submitted to the meeting for approval and, if approved, are signed by the chairman. The parochial church council then publishes them by exhibiting them at the principal door of every church and building licensed for worship and at such other conspicuous places as it thinks appropriate (R.8 (2) and (3)).

APPOINTMENT OF AUDITORS

The meeting appoints the auditors to the parochial church council but if it fails to do so the parochial church council appoints them (R.8 (5), App. II, i (g)).

BUSINESS INITIATED BY OTHER PERSONS

Any person entitled to attend may ask any question about parochial church matters or bring about a discussion of any matter of general or parochial church interest. A suitable method in the latter case is to move a resolution either in general terms or making recommendations to the parochial church council in relation to its duties. Such a resolution, if passed, would be a recommendation only and would not be binding on the parochial church council (R.8 (6)). Resolutions may be moved by private persons or on behalf of some body or organisation in the parish.

ELECTIONS

Three elections are required to be held at annual meetings. In 1976 and every third year afterwards the parochial representatives on the deanery synod are elected. Every year representatives of the laity on the parochial church council are elected. Every year sidesmen are elected. The elections must be held in this order. It is important that the representatives in the deanery synod should be known before voting takes place for the council as they are *ex officio* members of the council and should not therefore stand (R.8 (4)). Elections to the diocesan synod are held at deanery level.

QUALIFICATIONS FOR ELECTIONS

In all three elections candidates must be persons whose names are on the electoral roll and they must either have consented to serve or the meeting must be of opinion that there is sufficient evidence of their willingness to serve. There are no further qualifications required for a sidesman. There is no special age qualification for a representative on the parochial church council, so he must be 17 or over which is the qualifying age for entry on the roll. A candidate for the deanery synod must be at least 18.

A candidate for the council must be an actual communicant member of the Church of England or of a Church in communion with the Church of England. A member of either such Church must have communicated at a service of the Church of England or of a Church in communion with the Church of England at least three times in the past twelve months. Thus, for example, a member of the Church of England would be qualified if he had been in Canada and communicated there, and a Canadian would be qualified whether he had communicated here or in Canada. A candidate for the deanery synod must be an actual communicant of the Church of England, though he also could count occasions when he had communicated outside England at a service of a Church in communion with the Church of England.

While communicant members of Churches not in communion with the Church of England are admitted to Church of England altars as individuals they are not thereby qualified as members of the Church of England or of Churches in communion with the Church of England. An actual communicant member of the Church of England must be confirmed or ready and desirous of being confirmed and a communicant member of a Church in communion with the Church of England must be of communicant status in that Church. Only in very exceptional cases could a member of a Church not in communion with the Church of England have grounds for claiming the necessary qualifications for standing for these elections.

If a person has his name entered on the roll of more than one parish he may stand for election to the councils of all these parishes but he must choose one parish only for the purpose of election to a deanery synod (R.1 (3)).

The diocesan registrar for special reasons is disqualified from standing for election to a parochial church council or a deanery synod in his diocese (R.9 and R.44 (1)).

CONDUCT OF ELECTIONS

All three elections are conducted in the same way. There used to be a special method for sidesmen, but this has been abolished. The only difference now is that clergymen entitled to attend the annual meeting may nominate, second and vote in elections for sidesmen. In the other two elections only those whose names are on the roll may nominate, second or vote. A candidate may be nominated and seconded in writing before the meeting or verbally at the meeting. If the number of candidates is no more than the seats to be filled they are declared elected. Otherwise a vote must be taken. All those entitled to vote have as many votes as there are seats to be filled but may not give more than one vote to any one candidate. Voting must take place at the meeting, and a poll may no longer be demanded, as used to be possible. Voting may be by show of hands, if no person objects, but this method is obviously inappropriate where there is a number of seats to be filled. Otherwise it is by voting papers. These must be signed since that provides the only check on the eligibility of the voter. In some parishes objection is taken to the necessity for signing. It is possible for the signature to be on a detachable slip and torn off before counting, but in that case it is essential that there should be the same mark on both parts of the original document so that if a voter's eligibility is challenged his voting paper can be identified. If there is a tie by two or more candidates for the last place or places there is no casting vote in the chairman but the matter is decided by lot (R.10 (1)–(8)).

PUBLICATION OF RESULTS

The results of the elections must be announced as soon as practicable by the person presiding over them and a notice of the results bearing the date when they were announced must be displayed at the principal door of every church and building licensed for public worship in the parish for not less than 14 days. Returns of those elected to the deanery synod must be sent to the secretary of that synod. (R.10 (9) and (10).)

APPEALS

If anyone objects to the allowance or disallowance of a vote or the result of an election or other choice he may appeal to the rural dean, or if there is no rural dean to the archdeacon, within 14 days of the allowance or disallowance or the announcement of the result of the election by the presiding officer. An error in the roll is not a ground of appeal against an election result unless it has already been decided that there is an error or the question was already the subject of an appeal and the error would be material to the result. The allowance or disallowance of a vote is not a ground of appeal against the result of an election unless it would be material to the result. Unless agreement is reached the matter is referred to an electoral commission appointed by the diocesan synod, which hears the case and must give parties a right to appear in person or through a legal or other representative. (R.36).

SPECIAL PAROCHIAL CHURCH MEETING

The minister may summon a special parochial church meeting and must do so if he receives a written request from not less than one-third of the members of the parochial church council. The same procedure is followed as for annual meetings with any necessary modifications (R.18 (1)).

EXTRAORDINARY MEETING

An extraordinary meeting convened by the archdeacon may also be held as a means of investigating difficulties in a parish. The convening and procedure are governed by Rule 18.

6. Choosing Churchwardens

The qualifications and method of election of representatives of the laity on the deanery synod and parochial church council and of sidesmen, have been discussed, but nothing has yet been said about churchwardens. They are not chosen at the annual meeting but at a special meeting which normally precedes it. The law is contained in the Churchwardens (Appointment and Resignation) Measure 1964, sections of which are referred to by C. and a number and the Church Representation Rules. Only minimum changes to the 1964 Measure were made by the Rules and it was recognised that it would probably require scrutiny at a convenient moment to bring it into closer accord with developments since 1964.

QUALIFICATIONS AND NUMBER

The office of churchwarden dates from a time when it was expected that everyone would be a member of the Church of England. Every householder of full age, whether male or female, except aliens, Jews or persons convicted of felony, perjury or fraud was eligible and was usually bound to serve if appointed. Every parish was required to have churchwardens and it occasionally happened that someone who was not a member of the Church of England was chosen. The Churchwardens (Appointment and Resignation) Measure provided that churchwardens must be members of the Church of England and have communicated at least three times in the past year in the Church of England or a Church in communion with the Church of England, except where the bishop otherwise permits, must be at least 21 and must be either resident in the parish or have their names on the church electoral roll. No person is to be chosen unless he has signified consent to serve. The persons mentioned above who were definitely disqualified remain disqualified. In future unless there is some special arrangement there are to be two churchwardens in every parish (C.1).

SPECIAL ARRANGEMENTS

There are all kinds of special arrangements about churchwardens in different parishes, as a result of private Acts of Parliament or statutory schemes or some ancient custom. Except over one matter which will be mentioned these special arrangements are preserved, but custom can only override the Measure if it has been in operation at least since 1925 (C.12 and 13). There is a special section about Guild Churches in the City of London (C.10).

MEETING OF THE PARISHIONERS

Originally elections were held at a meeting of the vestry which is a meeting of rate-payers whether resident in the parish or not. The 1964 Measure provides for a meeting of parishioners which may be attended by persons whose names are entered on the church electoral roll or who are resident in the parish and whose names are entered on a register of local government electors by reason of their residence (C.3). When there was a custom under which churchwardens were chosen by the vestry they were in future to be chosen by the meeting of the parishioners. If others chose jointly with the vestry they were to choose jointly with the meeting (C.12). The procedure for meetings is set out in the Measure and there will no longer be any need to look back into the ancient law. In general it is the same as for annual meetings. The meeting is convened by the minister or the churchwardens by a notice signed by the minister or a churchwarden. The notice states the place, day and hour of the meeting, and is posted on or near the principal door of the parish church and all other buildings licensed for public worship for a period including the last two Sundays before the meeting. The chair is taken by the minister if he is present or, if he is not, by a person chosen by the meeting. The chairman has a casting vote, except in elections of churchwardens. The meeting has power to adjourn and to determine its own rules of procedure, and appoints a clerk to take the minutes (C.3 and R.11 (2) (c)).

TIME OF CHOOSING CHURCHWARDENS

Unless there was a custom to the contrary, Canon Law provided that the meeting must take place in Easter week, though it was held that elections held round about Easter time but not in Easter week were valid though irregular. The 1964 Measure provided that meetings may be held any time from 1st January to the end of the week following Easter week, as for annual meetings. The Synodical Government Measure substitutes 30th April to conform with the change for annual meetings (R.11).

MANNER OF CHOOSING CHURCHWARDENS

Canon 89 of the Canons of 1603 set out the old law on the method of choosing churchwardens. ' All Churchwardens or Questmen in every parish shall be chosen by the joint consent of the Minister and the Parishioners, if it may be: but if they cannot agree upon such a choice, then the Minister shall choose one and the Parishioners another.' This law applied unless there was a custom to the contrary. In fact very often failure to agree was assumed and the minister chose one churchwarden and the meeting the other. When the 1964 Measure was being prepared it was considered whether the practice in so many parishes should be adopted as the normal procedure, but it was decided that the procedure of joint consent in the Canon had much to commend it and ought to be followed. The old law was repeated in modern form and machinery was put into the Measure to ensure that it was properly carried out. The Measure provides that an attempt should be made to choose by joint consent, which should be shown by a motion stating the name or names of persons to be chosen being declared to have been carried, and by the minister giving his consent to the person or persons named either before the putting of the motion or immediately after the declaration of the result. If both churchwardens have not been chosen in this way, then the procedure by joint consent is regarded as having failed. If there is no joint consent the minister appoints his churchwarden first and the other is then elected by the meeting. If there is no minister the meeting elects both churchwardens. If there is a casual vacancy among churchwardens the new churchwarden is chosen in the same manner as the person who caused the casual vacancy (C.2).

It might be worth mentioning here that the terms ' vicar's warden ' and ' people's warden ' are not known to the law and the position and rights of churchwardens however chosen are the same.

Usually if the procedure by joint consent is used exactly the right number of candidates are put forward. If there is a contest it is probably desirable to regard joint consent as having failed and for one churchwarden to be chosen by the minister and one by the meeting. Alternatively an informal election could be held of all candidates approved by the minister and then the motions required by the Measure containing the names of the successful candidates would be moved. If motions are moved without the preliminary stage of an election it could happen that both places could be filled before an opportunity had been given to test the feelings of the meeting on a candidate who might in fact be preferred.

When elections are held either because there has been no joint consent or because there is no minister the procedure for elections at annual meetings is followed. Clergymen may nominate and vote as well as lay persons entitled to attend the meeting, but this does not apply to the minister, as, if he is present, he has already chosen one churchwarden.

ADMISSION

After election and before entering upon their duties church-wardens are required to be admitted to office and the 1964 Measure requires that at a time and place to be fixed by the ordinary, who may be either the bishop or the archdeacon, each person chosen to be a churchwarden must appear before the ordinary or his substitute and be admitted. Before doing so he must subscribe the declaration that he will faithfully and diligently perform the duties of his office and must make the declaration in the presence of the ordinary or his substitute. Admissions generally take place at visitations, but if a churchwarden cannot be present then special arrangements should be made for his admission. Having been admitted churchwardens continue in office until their successors are admitted. If a churchwarden is chosen for a second year, he should be admitted again even though he would continue if he was not admitted (C.7).

The churchwarden used to have no right to resign although a meeting of parishioners such as appointed him could accept his resignation if it decided to do so. The 1964 Measure gave him the right to resign provided that the minister and any other churchwarden consented and the bishop accepted his resignation. He resigns in writing to the bishop. The churchwarden ceases to be a churchwarden if he is neither resident in the parish nor has his name on the roll. If he removes his name from the roll but still resides in the parish, he must resign if he wants to cease to be a churchwarden (C.8 and 9).

7. The Parochial Church Council

Membership of a parochial church council is of three kinds—
ex officio, elected and co-opted.

EX OFFICIO MEMBERS

The minister and all licensed assistant curates of the parish were
and still are members. The 1969 Rules added vicars in a team
ministry involving the parish. If the parish is part of a group
ministry all the incumbents in the group receive papers and can
attend and speak. They are not however members and cannot
vote. This right does not apply to other clergy in the group.

Churchwardens are members provided their names are on the
roll and they have communicated at least three times during the
past year in the Church of England or another Church in communion with the Church of England.

Deaconesses and women workers licensed to the parish or a
male lay worker licensed to the parish and receiving payment for
pastoral work in the parish are *ex officio* members. So also is a
reader whose name is on the roll provided the annual meeting so
decides. This decision may be made in respect of all readers or a
particular individual or class of readers.

Lay members of any deanery or diocesan synod or General
Synod whose names are on the roll of the parish are *ex officio*
members (R.12 (1) and (3)). When a person is on the roll of
more than one parish he is only an *ex officio* member for the
parish which he has chosen to qualify for membership of such
synod (R.1 (3)). Lay members of a deanery synod hold office
from the date of their election until the 31st May following the
election of their successors. For a short period the old and new
members of the synod will overlap on the council. This is
convenient because the new members take office in the Synod on
the 31st May not when they are elected.

ELECTED MEMBERS

The number of the elected members is decided by the annual meeting and may be altered by resolution of the annual meeting. The alteration cannot take effect until the next annual meeting (R.12 (1)). Elected members hold office until the end of the next annual meeting unless the meeting decides that members of the council should serve for three years in which case one-third only should retire each year. In that event those who have been longest in office retire, and if it is necessary to decide between persons elected on the same day, the decision must be taken by lot, unless they reach agreement among themselves. In any case no one may hold office without re-election for longer than three years (R.14). Usually retiring representatives are eligible for re-election if still qualified. There is however power for the annual meeting to decide that no one may be a representative for more than a specified number of years continuously. It can also decide that after a specified interval a member can stand again (R.15). If a representative's name is removed from the roll he automatically retires from the council, unless he becomes a co-opted member or unless his name is removed at his own request, in which case he can only retire if the parochial church council resolves that he may. The reason for this exception is that the parochial church council is a corporate body with financial responsibility (R.12 (2)). If there is a casual vacancy among the elected members, it can be filled by the council (R.39 (1)).

CO-OPTED MEMBERS

The parochial church council may co-opt members not exceeding in number one-fifth of the elected members. They must be clergymen or lay members of the Church of England who are at least 17 years old and who have communicated at least three times in the past year in the Church of England or a Church in communion with it. They need not have their names on the roll. Their term of office ends at the conclusion of the annual meeting following their co-option but they may be co-opted again (R.12 (1)).

The question is sometimes raised whether a person receiving payment from the council, such as an organist or verger can be a member of it. Legally there is nothing to prevent it, but it is obviously a factor which ought to be considered, and the membership of such persons might in some circumstances be undesirable.

The proceedings of the parochial church council are not invalidated by any vacancy in the membership or by any member not being properly qualified or elected (R.App. II 16).

SPECIAL ARRANGEMENTS

If there are two or more churches or other buildings licensed for worship in a parish the annual meeting can make a scheme either apportioning the representatives on the council so that all congregations are properly represented or for the election of a district church council for any building including the parish church itself and the area around it, or for both purposes. The scheme for a district church council makes provision for the election of representatives of the laity, for *ex officio* members and for the chairmanship of the council and can contain other appropriate provisions on membership and procedure. The scheme may delegate functions of the parochial church council to the district church council and subject to the scheme the parochial church council can itself decide to delegate other functions. The scheme may also provide for the election or choice of one or two deputy churchwardens for any building and can delegate the functions of the churchwardens to them. Subject to the scheme the churchwardens themselves can delegate further functions. Schemes require a two-thirds majority of those present and voting at the annual meeting and come into operation in the following year. They must be sent when approved to the secretary of the diocesan synod. If he is doubtful about a scheme he can lay it before the bishop's council and standing committee of the diocesan synod which can veto it.

The Pastoral Measure 1968 makes provision for district church councils, deputy churchwardens, parishes with two parish churches, joint parochial church councils acting for more than one parish and group councils which can act for certain purposes for all parishes in a group (R.16 (6) and 17).

PROCEDURE

The procedure of parochial church councils is governed by rules set out in Appendix II to the Church Representation Rules. A parochial church council may vary these rules if it obtains the consent of the diocesan synod (R.13). In the following paragraphs the figures in brackets not preceded by a letter refer to paragraphs in this Appendix.

OFFICERS

The minister is chairman and a lay member elected by the parochial church council is vice-chairman. In the absence of the chairman the vice-chairman has all the powers of the chairman. The parochial church council appoints its secretary who need not be a member and may be paid a remuneration. His duties are to keep the minutes, to have charge of the documents relating to the current business of the council other than the roll and to keep the secretaries of the diocesan and deanery synods informed as to his name and address. The council may appoint a treasurer, but if it does not do so the churchwardens act as such. The treasurer must not be paid. It appoints a church electoral roll officer who can be a member or the secretary or some other person and may pay him if he is not a member. He has charge of the electoral roll. It appoints the auditors, if the annual meeting has not done so or if those appointed are unwilling to act (1).

MEETINGS

Not less than four meetings must be held in a year, and if only four are held they must be roughly at quarterly intervals (2). The parochial church council, or the chairman if it does not do so, decides the place of meeting (9). The chairman may convene a meeting at any time, and if he does not do so within seven days after a request signed by at least one-third of the members those members may convene a meeting (3). At least ten clear days before an ordinary meeting a notice stating the time and place of the meeting and signed by or on behalf of the chairman or members convening the meeting must be posted at the principal door of every church or building licensed for worship. Not less than seven days before the meeting the secretary sends a notice signed by him or on his behalf to every member stating the time and place of the meeting and the agenda, including motions of which he has received notice from any member (4).

PROCEDURE AT MEETINGS

The chairman, or failing him the vice-chairman, takes the chair but either may vacate it for a particular meeting or a particular item of business if he considers it desirable, and must do so if the meeting so resolves. In the absence of both, the meeting elects its chairman (5). One-third of the members is a quorum. The business is taken in the order in which it appears on the agenda, unless the meeting decides to vary it, and no business not on the agenda may be taken without the consent of three-quarters of the members present (6, 7). The business is decided by a majority vote. In addition to his ordinary vote the chairman has a casting vote if necessary (10, 11). A meeting may adjourn to a time and place to be decided by the meeting (13).

EMERGENCY AND EXTRAORDINARY MEETINGS

If a matter arises requiring immediate action the chairman may convene an emergency meeting by giving three clear days' notice in writing to members. More than half the members must be present if business is to be transacted and only business set out in the notice may be transacted (8). It is also possible to hold an extraordinary meeting convened by the archdeacon, if there are difficulties in the parish (R.18).

MINUTES

The names of members present must be recorded. One-fifth of the members voting on a resolution may require that the names of those voting for and against it should be recorded. Any member may require that the way in which he voted on any resolution should be recorded. Members of the council, the bishop, persons authorized by him in writing and the archdeacon may have access to the minutes without the council's express authority but for access by others their authority is required. (12).

COMMITTEES

The council must have a standing committee of at least five persons. The minister and churchwardens who are members of the council are *ex officio* members. Other members, of whom there must be at least two, must be members of the council and are appointed and may be removed by the council. The committee has power to transact the business of the council between meetings but is bound by any directions given by the council (14). Other committees on various branches of church work in the parish may be appointed. The members need not be members of the council and the minister is an *ex officio* member of all committees (15).

Appendix—Forms

N.B. The forms contained in the Appendix ought to be used, but forms which have a substantially similar effect will be sufficient to avoid the action taken being invalid. Only the forms set out in the Measure affecting the parish are included. A new form of application for entry on the roll came into use in 1974 and changes were made in the other forms. The complete list of relevant forms obtainable from any church bookshop is as follows:—

Application for Enrolment on the Electoral Roll (SG 1), 45p per 100. *

Annual Meeting Pack SG ' A ', 24p for three copies of each form.
   †Revision of Electoral Roll/Preparation of New Roll, (SG 4/9)
   †Notice of Annual Parochial Church Meeting, (SG 20)
   Election of Churchwardens, (SG 21)
   Result of Elections, (SG 24)

Church Electoral Roll Certificate (SG 7), 7p for 3; 10p for 6.

Nomination Form, (SG 22), 16p for 25.

Voting Paper, (SG 23), 47p per 100.

P.C.C. Meeting Notice (SG 30), 24p for 25.

P.C.C. Agenda Form (SG 31), 34p per 100.

* The new version is shown overleaf but as there are considerable stocks of the earlier printing they are continuing to be sold with instructions about necessary deletions.

† Owing to the nature of the packaging it is not practicable to substitute the new forms (SG 4 and SG 20) but they can be obtained in 1974 from either the Church Information Office, Church House, Dean's Yard, London SW1P 3NZ or from SPCK, 7 Castle Street Reading, Berks. RG1 7SB. Three copies of each price 10p including postage.

APPLICATION FOR ENROLMENT ON THE CHURCH ELECTORAL ROLL

I ....
(Full Christian name and surname)

of ....
(Full postal address)
am baptised and am a member of the Church of England or of a Church in communion with it. I am seventeen years or over and am either resident in the parish or have habitually attended public worship there for at least the past six months.

I apply for entry on the church electoral roll of the parish of

....

Signed....................................

Date....................................

NOTES

1. The only Churches at present in communion with the Church of England are other Anglican Churches and certain foreign Churches. Members of other Churches in England are usually admitted to communion as individuals, but their Churches are not yet in communion with the Churches of England. Such persons would naturally take part in the government of their own Churches.

2. Every six years a new roll is prepared and those on the previous roll are informed so that they can re-apply. If you are not resident in the parish but were on the roll as an habitual worshipper and have been prevented by sickness or absence or other essential reason from worshipping for the past six months, you may write 'would' before 'have habitually attended' in the form and add 'but was prevented from doing so because . . .' and then state the reason.

3. If you have any problems over this form, please approach the clergy or lay people responsible for the parish, who will be pleased to help you.   [New form SG1

REVISION OF CHURCH ELECTORAL ROLL

Diocese of

Parish of

NOTICE IS HEREBY GIVEN

that the church electoral roll of the above parish will be revised by the parochial church council,

*beginning on   the   day of   19

and ending on   the   day of   19

After such revision a copy of the roll will forthwith be exhibited on, or near to, the principal door of the parish church for inspection.

Under the Church Representation Rules any persons are entitled to have their names entered on the roll if they:

(i) are baptized;

(ii) are members of the Church of England or of any Church in communion with the Church of England;

(iii) are seventeen or over;

(iv) are resident in the parish, or, not being resident in the parish, have habitually attended public worship in the parish during the six months before the date of application for enrolment; and

(v) have signed a form of application for enrolment.

Forms of application for enrolment can be obtained from the undersigned and should be returned, if possible, in time for the revision.

Any error discovered in the roll should at once be reported to the undersigned.

Dated this†   day of   19

Church Electoral Roll Officer

Address

*NOTE—The Revision must be completed not less than 15 days or more than 28 days before the Annual Parochial Church Meeting.   †Not less than 14 days' notice must be given.

SPCK–Mowbrays/Church Information Office
Design © Central Board of Finance, 1970
For 1974 only, not available through bookshops

SG 4

PREPARATION OF NEW ROLL

Diocese of ....

Parish of ....

* NOTE—
The new roll
must be
completed
not less than
15 days or
more than
28 days
before the
Annual
Parochial
Church
Meeting.

Notice is hereby given that under the Church Representation Rules a new Church Electoral Roll is being prepared. All persons who wish to have their names entered on the new Roll, whether their names are entered on the present Roll or not, are requested to apply for enrolment if possible not later than...

The new roll will come into operation on

....

Forms of application for enrolment can be obtained from the undersigned.

Under the Church Representation Rules any persons are entitled to have their names entered on the Roll, if they:—

(i) are baptised,

(ii) are members of the Church of England or of any Church in communion with the Church of England,

(iii) are seventeen or over,

(iv) are resident in the parish, or, not being resident in the **parish** have habitually attended public worship in the parish during the **six** months before the date of application for enrolment, and

(v) have signed a form of application for enrolment.

Any error discovered on the roll should at once be reported to the undersigned.

Dated this ....day of ....19......

....
Church Electoral Roll Officer

New form SG 9]   Address.......................................

NOTICE OF ANNUAL PAROCHIAL CHURCH MEETING

Parish of

THE ANNUAL PAROCHIAL CHURCH MEETING will be held in

on   the   day

of   19   at   am/pm

For the election of parochial representatives of the laity as follows:

*to the deanery synod   representatives

to the parochial church council   representatives

For the election of sidesmen.
For the consideration of:
a/ A copy or copies of the roll;
b/ An annual report on the proceedings of the council;
c/ An annual report on the financial affairs of the parish;
d/ The audited accounts of the council for the year
ending on the 31st December immediately preceding the
meeting;
e/ An audited statement of the funds and property of the
council;
f/ A report upon the fabric, goods, and ornaments of
the church or churches of the parish;
g/ A report on the proceedings of the deanery synod;
and other matters of parochial or general church interest.

All persons whose names are entered upon the church electoral roll of the parish (and such persons only) are entitled to vote at the election of parochial representatives of the laity.

A person is qualified to be elected a parochial representative of the laity to the deanery synod if—
(a) his name is entered on the church electoral roll of the parish;
(b) he is a member of the Church of England who is confirmed or ready and desirous of being confirmed and has received Communion according to the use of the Church of England or a Church in communion with the Church of England at least three times during the twelve months preceding the date of the election; and
(c) he is of 18 years or upwards.

A person is qualified to be elected a parochial representative of the laity to the parochial church council if—
(a) his name is entered on the church electoral roll of the parish; and
(b) he is a member of the Church of England who is confirmed or ready and desirous of being confirmed or a communicant member of a Church in communion with the Church of England and has received Communion according to the use of the Church of England or a Church in communion with the Church of England at least three times during the twelve months preceding the date of the election.

Any person whose name is on the roll may be a sidesman.

† Dated   19   Signed

(‡Minister of the Parish)

*Include where applicable.
†See Rule 6 (1). The notice must be affixed for a period including the last two Sundays before the day of the meeting.

‡Or vice-chairman of the parochial church council, as the case may be. (See Rule 6 (3) of the Church Representation Rules.)

SPCK-Mowbrays/Church Information Office
Design © Central Board of Finance 1970
For 1974 only, not available through local shops.

SG 20

PART III—FINANCE AND PROPERTY

It seems desirable to consider financial and property questions as part of the information required before considering the work of the parish.

Reference has been made to benefice stipends and property in Chapter 3, and from the point of view of the laity these can more easily be considered as relevant to their duty of support of the clergy. (See Chapter 13.) The whole question of the ownership of and other rights and duties in connection with the church building, the contents of the church and the churchyard are a subject on their own. (See Chapters 16 and 17.)

This part then deals with the place of the parochial church council and with trusts held by incumbents and churchwardens. Property law is often extremely technical and this is certainly so with these matters. Full details of the legislation involved are not given, and what is written may well not be easily understood. Property dealings require expert advice from lawyers or officials of the diocesan board of finance or others who have practical experience of transactions of this kind.

It is emphasised that only the Church's own law is covered in this section not the effect of secular law on the Church, a very wide subject certainly requiring expert advice.

8. Parochial Church Council Finance and Property

In this Chapter a P. with a number after it is in reference to that section of the Parochial Church Councils (Powers) Measure, 1956.

A BODY CORPORATE

The parochial church council is a body corporate, and its existence is not affected by any changes in membership. It can hold property but the Measure restricts its power to do so. The council's documents must be signed or signed and sealed by the chairman who presided at the meeting when the decision authorising the execution of the document was made and by two members who were present at it. This can be done either at or after the meeting (P.3).

The council is the financial authority of the parish. It is responsible for collecting and administering the money required for church purposes, and frames an annual budget. There are all kinds of methods of raising money. Many parishes have their system of stewardship. But these are matters outside the law. The law in fact refers only to two methods of raising money.

The first is collections at services. The alms taken at the Holy Communion service are allocated by the incumbent and church-wardens for charitable purposes as provided in the Book of Common Prayer. In fact they are usually treated as ordinary parish funds in these days, particularly where the Holy Communion service is the one usually attended by the congregation. Most purposes for which church funds are used are in fact charitable, so no difficulty arises. There are some exceptions like the insurance of buildings. Collections at other services are allocated jointly by the minister and the parochial church council. If there is disagreement the matter is referred to the bishop who gives directions.

The second method referred to in the Measure is the collection of a voluntary church rate, which can be undertaken by the parochial church council. Before 1868 a compulsory church rate could be levied similar to a local authority rate and the amount calculated had to be paid. Now there can be no compulsion, but this method of raising money is occasionally used in city areas on a voluntary basis (P.4 (1), 7, 9 (3)).

HOLDING OF PROPERTY

The parochial church council may acquire property for church purposes connected with the parish, for instance a house for a curate or verger, or for investment, either for general expenses or some special purpose, or in connection with ' educational schemes ', that is schemes for the ' spiritual, moral and physical training of persons residing in or near the parish '. Normally the management of such property rests with the council, but it has certain powers of delegation to school managers or trustees

F
73

if the property is held in connection with an educational scheme. The Department of Education and Science or the local authority are sometimes willing to give grants, but they cannot do so unless they can be assured that the property will continue to be used for the agreed purposes. Therefore the council is given power to enter into undertakings which will be binding on the council in the future when its membership may have changed. Ordinarily undertakings are not binding on succeeding councils, and this is a point that councils should bear in mind. The power to hold property in connection with an educational scheme cannot be exercised without the consent of the diocesan education committee (P.5).

Inevitably parochial church councils vary very much in their capacity to manage property. Flourishing town parishes would have no difficulty at all, but in small country parishes it might lay a heavy burden on the members of the parochial church council if they had no assistance or supervision, and they might perhaps become involved in serious trouble or expense. The same law has to apply to all and therefore the Measure provides that there should be certain safeguards. These safeguards only apply to specified kinds of property, namely, all interests in land except for leases for a term not exceeding a year, even though the term may be renewable after such a period without any fresh agreement, and all personal property held on permanent trusts, that is property where the capital is to be held indefinitely and only the income used. Any question whether property is held on permanent trusts is decided by a person appointed by the bishop. The safeguard is provided by bringing in the diocesan board of finance or other equivalent body. The parochial church council cannot acquire such property without the consent of the diocesan body, and when it has been acquired the diocesan body becomes the legal owner and the property cannot be sold, let, exchanged or charged, nor can legal proceedings be taken over it without that body's consent. Subject to these safeguards the parochial church council has full right of management. Other property, that is leases for the short periods mentioned, investments held temporarily and current money can be acquired, owned and dealt with without reference to the diocesan body (P.6). The consent of the Charity Commissioners or Department of Education and Science is not required for transactions where property is vested in the diocesan body, nor where property is used exclusively as a place of worship, a burial ground, a Sunday school, a church hall, a residence for a clergyman, nor for any ground surrounding such property.

9. Incumbents and Churchwardens' Property

The powers of the parochial church council for the holding and management of property and the limitations upon those powers have just been described. Incumbents, churchwardens, and incumbents and churchwardens jointly are often trustees of charitable trusts. In 1960 a Charities Act was passed which placed certain obligations upon trustees, for instance an obligation to be registered with the Charity Commissioners and to send in accounts to them. The Act also provided that the Charity Commissioners could ' except ' charities from these requirements. It was considered that it was preferable that some of these trusts should be supervised by the diocesan body rather than by the Charity Commissioners and a new Measure called the Incumbents and Churchwardens (Trusts) Measure 1964 gave to a diocesan body similar powers over these trusts as they have over parochial church council property. I. followed by a number in this Chapter refers to that section of the Measure.

The Measure was complicated by the fact that, while the rules for parochial church councils' property had always applied during the comparatively short life of these councils, incumbents and churchwardens, on the other hand, already held and sometimes had held for a very long time, various trusts and other property. In altering the law account had to be taken of the past. A further difficulty was that while the incumbent was a corporation and therefore any property vested in him automatically passed to his successors, churchwardens were not. Strictly whenever there was a change of churchwarden, where the churchwarden was a trustee, an instrument of transfer had to be prepared. This was probably never done. As a result property which was regarded as belonging to successive churchwardens might belong at law to the personal representatives of long-dead churchwardens. One of the advantages of the Measure is that the diocesan body which has a continuous existence has an interest in all these trusts and, whatever changes might take place at the parochial level, the diocese knows about the trusts, is able to take action and regularise difficult situations, and ensures that trust property is not lost, as sometimes used to happen.

TRUSTEES TO WHOM THE MEASURE APPLIES

In general these are the incumbent, churchwardens, the incumbent and churchwardens jointly, and any of these persons holding property as joint trustees with another ' ecclesiastical corporation sole ', which means in effect a bishop or an archdeacon. If some person who is not mentioned in this list is a joint trustee then the Measure does not apply to that trust. The Measure covers cases where everyone imagines that the churchwardens are trustees but where in fact the necessary legal formalities have not been carried out. So it is provided that the Measure should apply to trusts where the persons acting as trustees are the persons mentioned, even if they are not validly appointed. Sometimes the parochial church council in fact administers trusts which are properly churchwardens' trust, and it is provided that in that case also the Measure should apply. But if the terms of the trust make it quite clear that it is not intended that the churchwardens should act as trustees but they have been acting contrary to the intentions of the trust, then the Measure does not apply, but the matter should be sorted out in some other way so that the intentions of the trust are as nearly as possible carried out (I.2 (I)).

PROPERTY TO WHICH THE MEASURE APPLIES

The Measure applies only to trusts for ecclesiastical purposes, not for instance to a trust for the provision of food or fuel to the poor. Such trusts are properly a matter for the Charity Commissioners, not the Church. The Measure only applies to an estate or interest in land or an interest in personal property held or to be held on permanent trusts. If any question arises as to whether personal property comes within the Measure it is decided by a person appointed by the bishop in the same way as for parochial church council property. Certain property is excluded from the Measure including the rights of the incumbent in a church, churchyard, burial ground or the endowments of his benefice, the rights of the churchwardens in the goods, ornaments and moveables of the church, personal chattels such as, for instance, a car, property held on educational trusts and leases for a term not exceeding a year (I.2).

PROCEDURE FOR VESTING PROPERTY

Where the Measure applies to any trust the trustees must let the diocesan body know in writing. If a diocesan body knows of any such trust, whether they are told by the trustees or not, it must take the necessary action to vest the property in itself. Procedure is laid down by the Measure and there are provisions for notice to all interested parties and the Charity Commissioners. The actual vesting is made by a declaration of the diocesan body which can cover any number of trusts belonging to any number of trustees, thus saving expense (I.3 and Schedule). By now presumably most if not all existing trusts have been transferred. Newly created trusts should provide that the property should be held in accordance with the Measure without the necessity for a declaration.

OTHER PROVISIONS OF THE MEASURE

Neither an incumbent nor churchwardens nor an incumbent and churchwardens may acquire as trustees any property to which this Measure applies, other than an interest in personal property by gift or under a will, without the consent of the diocesan body. When any property is vested in the diocesan body the present trustees remain managing trustees but they may not sell, lease, let, exchange or charge or take any legal proceedings in relation to the property without the consent of the diocesan body, which in the case of legal proceedings, may be given by an agent of the body (I. 4, 5).

RECORDS OF PROPERTY

By Canon F.17 incumbents and churchwardens must keep records of all lands, goods, and other possessions of churches and chapels in accordance with instructions and forms laid down by the General Synod.

PART IV—THE LIFE OF THE PARISH

10. Church Services

It will be something of a relief for most readers as for the author to get past the technicalities of machinery, finance and property to the life of the parish. The right beginning is the worship of the Church.

PERMITTED SERVICES

Until 1965 the law relating to services was extremely strict. The Prayer Book services were supposed to be used universally with only a little carefully controlled power of variation. Special forms of service could be authorised by the bishop, but these could strictly contain nothing except passages from the Bible and the Prayer Book, hymns or anthems and an address. A clergyman who introduced an unauthorised variation into a Prayer Book service or conducted another service with prayers from sources other than the Prayer Book acted illegally. Of course the law was not kept in most, if any, parishes.

A Measure called the Prayer Book (Alternative and Other Services) Measure 1965, the substance of which is found in Canons B.1 to B.5 made sense of the situation and introduced important new reforms. If Parliament agrees this Measure will shortly be replaced by the Church of England (Worship and Doctrine) Measure and revised versions of Canons B1 to B5 will come into operation.

First, experimental services alternative to those in the Prayer Book can be authorised by the General Synod. A two-thirds majority in each House of the Synod is required to make sure the service is generally acceptable. For most services two alternative forms have been authorised, Series 1 and 2. Series 1 was brought quickly into force to permit accepted existing practices which had previously been illegal. Many of these had been already approved by the Church when the Prayer Book Measures were presented to

Parliament in the late 1920s only to have Parliament reject them. Series 2 services were then approved for services other than Marriage and Burial. In 1972 Series 3 Holy Communion was approved, and the Series 3 Burial Service was published in 1973. Series 3 departs further from the traditional than Series 2 for instance by addressing God as ' you ' instead of ' thou '.

An alternative form cannot be authorised for longer than seven years and must therefore be reconsidered during the period of authorisation if it is not to cease to be used. By about 1980 the power to authorise any alternative will cease.

The Church of England (Worship and Doctrine) Measure, if passed, will enable the General Synod to approve, amend, continue or discontinue forms of service, and there is no time limit either in the operation of the provisions or in the period of approval of a form of service. The Synod would thus be able to order the future worship of the Church without the need to go to Parliament. There is however one limitation on its powers. Should it at some future time decide that there should be new forms of service which should replace the 1662 forms then it must go to Parliament for authority to discontinue their use. Otherwise the 1662 forms must remain available for parishes that wish to use them. In fact there never has been any intention to propose discontinuance of the 1662 forms and the majority of diocesan synods considered that the Synod should have authority to decide this issue without going to Parliament. But there was a minority of some substance and in these circumstances the Synod decided that it should not assume this power.

In July 1973 the Synod considered the future course of liturgical revision and reached certain conclusions. Further Series 3 services should be prepared, but Series 1 and Series 2 forms should remain in use unless there was no real demand for them. Further consideration was to be given to a proposal to replace Series 1 and Series 2 Holy Communion services by a new form. Consideration should also be given to the preparation of a People's Service Book, which should contain all authorised forms of Morning and Evening Prayer and Holy Communion, with psalms, collects, epistles and gospels. Such a book would meet the ordinary needs of the churchgoer wherever he went. Whether it would also be appropriate to include the forms for baptism, confirmation, marriage and funerals was a matter that required consideration. At some future date the Synod should have the opportunity to decide whether a new Prayer Book should be authorised. If it were, then the 1662 services would either be incorporated into it or remain as alternatives.

Both the Convocations, and under the new Measure also the archbishops, in their provinces, and the bishops in their dioceses have power to authorise forms of service for occasions for which no provision is made by the Book of Common Prayer.

No form of service mentioned in the preceding paragraphs may be contrary to or indicative of any departure from the doctrine of the Church of England. The new Measure adds the words ' in any essential matter '. These words are necessary because there may be a proper desire to express new insights or differences of emphasis, but these must not be contrary to anything that is essential to the faith. The authority of the Book of Common Prayer as one of the doctrinal formularies of the Church is clearly affirmed in the Measure.

The clergyman taking a Prayer Book service or any other service authorised under the Measure has discretion to make variations which are not of substantial importance. He can also use his own forms of service for occasions on which no other provision is made. Anything that he does by virtue of these discretions must be reverent and seemly and doctrinally sound. If there is any doubt on these points, or whether a variation is or is not of substantial importance, the matter may be referred to the bishop for his pastoral guidance and advice. In serious cases discipline proceedings can be taken.

CONTROL OF SERVICES

Subject to the law, and to rights of consent or objection contained in the law, the incumbent has the control of services in the churches of his parish. But the 1965 Measure provides that service alternative to those contained in the Book of Common Prayer should not be used without the consent of the parochial church council. He can however use the 1662 Book without consent even if it means discontinuing other services which are in current use in the parish. Equally the parochial church council can require the use of the 1662 Book by refusing or withdrawing its consent to other forms of service.

The new Measure provides that the choice between the 1662 and any other authorised forms of service should be taken jointly by the incumbent and the parochial church council. There is thus to be partnership, instead of a legal right of initiative with the incumbent. In practice however it is likely that the initiative will be taken by the incumbent, even though either party can do so. If there is failure to agree then the parochial church council can require the use of new forms of service in regular use during at least two of the past four years either to the exclusion of or in addition to the 1662 forms. If there are no such services or the parochial church council does not exercise this option the 1662 forms must be used.

Here is an example of how this provision might operate. For three years a parish has used Series 2 Holy Communion. It decides to try Series 3. After six months either the incumbent or the parochial church council decides to discontinue the use of Series 3. Because Series 2 has been used for more than two years in the past four, the council can require the use of Series 2 either alone or with the periodic use of 1662. Otherwise 1662 must be used.

Under the 1965 Measure the minister decides which form of the occasional offices of baptism, marriage or burial, should be used but the persons concerned, such as the parents of a child to be baptised or the couple to be married, could ask him to use a particular form, though they could not require him to do so. They could however object beforehand to the use of any form other than the 1662 form, which the minister has the right to use if he wishes. It was not intended that the parochial church council should be involved, but the wording of the section inadvertently also requires its consent. Its general permission to use specified alternative forms should therefore be obtained. The new Measure follows the intention of the 1965 Measure omitting all reference to the parochial church council. It provides for the minister to decide subject to objection beforehand by the persons concerned, and this right of objection extends to all forms of service including the 1662 forms. If there is failure to agree the issue is referred to the bishop for his decision.

Whether or not the council has specific rights in connection with particular services, the council has a general right of discussing any questions which are or might be raised about the services and the wise incumbent pays attention to their advice and that of his congregation. It is usually right to involve laity more fully in the conduct of worship as is permitted or required in the new forms of service. When another person, clergyman or layman, is taking a service he must obey the law and the directions of the incumbent, but otherwise has the same right of ordering as the incumbent. Special services can be the creative act of clergy and laity together.

VESTURE OF MINISTERS

Canon B.8 lays down the appropriate vesture for clergymen to wear at services. It does not seem necessary to describe the law in detail in a book intended for laymen. It is made quite clear that the Church does not attach any particular doctrinal significance to the permitted diversities of vesture and certainly permission to use any particular vesture does not imply any doctrine not contained in the formularies of the Church of England.

If a clergyman wants to change the vesture ordinarily used in his church he must ascertain by consultation with the parochial church council that the change is acceptable. If a disagreement arises the matter must be dropped or referred to the bishop and his directions obeyed.

MORNING AND EVENING PRAYER

Morning and evening prayer must be said or sung in every parish church on Sundays and the principal feast and fast days. The bishop may make exceptions to this rule for good reason, but if either Morning or Evening Prayer is to be omitted for a period of more than three months the bishop must consult either the parochial church council or two members of it nominated by the council for the purpose. In daughter churches, unless special directions are given by the bishop, services are held at the discretion of the incumbent or priest in charge.

The clergy are expected to say Morning and Evening Prayer daily and should do so in church after tolling the bell.

Priests, deacons, deaconesses or readers may take either service. Nothing is said specifically about this matter in the Canon on women workers and their licences would make it clear if this was regarded as a normal part of their duties. In fact any lay person can receive the authority of the bishop to take either service at the invitation of the incumbent or, if he is not in a position to give it, of the churchwardens. As a last resort in a crisis the churchwardens can take a service or arrange for a suitable layman to do so without obtaining the authority of the bishop.

Only a priest can pronounce the absolution. Any other person taking the service should say the collect for the twenty-first Sunday after Trinity instead.

Any person clerical or lay, including members of other denominations, can preach provided they have authority either through the office they hold, or by licence or general permission from the bishop, or by a special permission given by him for the occasion.

Any person can read the lessons. This has been a long-standing practice though it was technically illegal until 1968. Certain lectionaries are authorised for use and any version of the Bible is permitted.

Documents to refer to on Morning and Evening Prayer are Canons B.11, B.11A, D.1 and E.4, and the Pastoral Measure 1968, section 74.

HYMNS AND MUSIC

The hymns and music at all services are subject to the final decision of the minister and must be appropriate and reverent. He must pay due heed to the advice and assistance of the organist (Canon B.20).

HOLY COMMUNION

The Holy Communion shall if practicable be celebrated in parish churches at least on all Sundays, principal feast days and Ash Wednesday. In daughter churches it is celebrated when convenient subject to the direction of the bishop (Canon B.14).

Holy Communion must be celebrated by a priest. Any person who has the authority of the bishop to do so may administer the bread and wine. The Convocations have approved a regulation which requires the incumbent or priest in charge of the church, or the rural dean if there is neither, supported by the church-wardens to apply in writing to the bishop if such authority is desired, giving relevant particulars. The person proposed must be baptised and confirmed. The bishop could appoint another bishop in the diocese or an archdeacon to act as his deputy for giving such permissions if he wished (Canon B.12).

Until the late 1960s it was considered inappropriate for a lay person to preach at Holy Communion, but now lay persons are permitted to preach in the same way as at Morning and Evening Prayer.

Subject to any directions by the bishop lay people can read the epistle and gospel. These are set out in the Prayer Book and until recently had to be read in that form. Now the Convocations with the concurrence of the House of Laity, in future the General Synod, may authorise other versions. The Revised Version, the Revised Standard Version, the New English Bible and the Jerusalem Bible have been authorised. (Canon B.12 and the Prayer Book (Versions of the Bible) Measure 1965).

Under the rubric at the end of the Confirmation service in the Prayer Book only those who are confirmed or ready and desirous of being confirmed should be admitted to receive Holy Communion. But in practice the law was never so interpreted by many and the bishops themselves made regulations on the subject.

A Commission on Intercommunion reported in 1968 and proposed considerable further relaxations. The matter came before the General Synod which decided upon a simpler more radical approach which is embodied in Canon B.15A, which came into operation in 1972.

Under this Canon there are two main paragraphs. The first relates to members of the Church of England. To be admitted to Holy Communion they must have been confirmed in the Church of England or be ready and desirous of being confirmed or have been episcopally confirmed in another Church with unction or with the laying on of hands. Thus for instance a confirmed Roman Catholic or member of an Orthodox Church who becomes a member of the Church of England is admitted without the need to be confirmed in the Church of England. The second paragraph relates to members of other Churches which subscribe to the doctrine of the Holy Trinity. They are admitted if they are baptised and communicants of good standing in their own Churches. It is emphasised that they are admitted by their own choice and any clergyman who refuses them communion is in breach of Canon Law. But if such a person continues to communicate regularly and appears likely to continue to do so the clergyman is to set before him the normal requirement of being confirmed. The duty of the clergyman is to mention the matter only, and he is not obliged to put any pressure. If he does so, but the person declines to be confirmed he must still be admitted to communion as of right. Baptised persons in danger of death are also to be admitted to Communion.

Canon B.15A, deals with admission to Holy Communion both of members of the Church of England and of members of other Churches. Members of the Church of England decide whether to communicate at services of other Churches which accept them, according to their own consciences. In 1973 the Synod considered the question of reciprocal intercommunion, that is, members of Churches sharing in a service arranged with this end in mind. It was agreed that as the situation was so fluid and the views of members differed so much no regulations were appropriate at the present time. The House of Bishops was requested to consider what guidance should be given.

It is the duty of confirmed persons to communicate regularly with proper preparation especially at Christmas, Easter and Whitsun (Canon B.15).

A person who is in malicious and open contention with his neighbours or in unrepented grave and open sin may be refused Communion. This is a matter for the bishop, but initially a parish clergyman may act if he considers it necessary (Canon B.16).

Holy Communion can be celebrated in places other than churches with the permission of the bishop. This permission is not necessary when giving Communion to the sick (Canon B.40).

It is the duty of the churchwardens with the advice and under the direction of the minister to provide the bread and wine. The bread can be leavened or unleavened and must be of best wheat flour. The wine must be fermented juice of the grape (Canon B.17).

BAPTISM AND CONFIRMATION

It is desirable that baptisms should be held at or immediately after a public service on a Sunday or other holy day, but they may be held on other days. Public baptisms are desirable so that ' the congregation there present may witness the receiving of them that be newly baptised into Christ's Church and be put in remembrance of their own profession made to God in their baptism ' (Canon B.21).

For the baptism of infants at least a week's notice must be given. The child of any resident or person on the Church electoral roll is to be accepted for baptism, but not of other persons unless the goodwill of the clergyman in whose parish they reside is obtained. If there is refusal or undue delay the parents or guardians can apply to the bishop. Refusal is not permitted provided the proper formalities are carried out. Delay is only permitted in order to prepare the parents or guardians or godparents.

Baptism is normally administered by a clergyman, but in the absence of a clergyman, a deaconess may baptise. Baptism in a private house by any person is sufficient but such baptisms ought only to be conducted for urgent reasons, and if possible a service of reception in church should follow (Canon B.22).

Godparents should be people who will fulfil their responsibilities by their care for the child and by giving a good example. The same responsibilities are laid on the parents whether or not they are also godparents, which they may be provided there is one other godparent. There must be one godfather and one godmother and there should be one other either godfather or godmother according to the sex of the child. There can be more than these if desired. Godparents must be baptised and should ordinarily be confirmed, but the minister can dispense with this requirement. A baptised member of another Church can therefore be a godparent if this dispensation is given (Canon B.23).

A person who has passed the stage of childhood may be baptised after instruction and proper preparation. He chooses two or three persons as his sponsors who have the qualifications required for godparents. They present him at the font and 'afterwards put him in mind of his Christian profession and duties'. The minister notifies the bishop and it is expected that the baptised person would wish to be confirmed as soon as possible (Canons B.23 and B.24).

Children who have been baptised should in due course be confirmed. They receive instruction and should be able to say the Creed, the Lord's Prayer and the Ten Commandments and to give an account of their faith as set out in the Catechism. There is now a greater emphasis on the need for a child to take personal responsibility for the decision to be confirmed than there used to be, and other methods of training for confirmation are in practice used, which should produce more effectively the same results as are the object of the traditional methods, namely that the person confirmed should understand the reality of the faith and act as required by it. A person can change his Christian name at confirmation (Canon B(27).

In 1971 a report on Christian Initiation was published. The General Synod will consider it again in 1974. Reactions indicate that it is a controversial report, and there can be no telling at this stage how far it will be accepted by the Synod. The Synod may wish to ascertain the views of diocesan synods. The following are the main proposals, which if accepted would lay greater stress on baptism and less stress on confirmation. The Church should make clear its recognition of baptism as the full and complete rite of Christian initiation and ordinarily baptism should be administered at the main service of the Church. A new service of Thanksgiving for the birth of a child should be prepared and be available if required, but it would not be a substitute for baptism as an initiation rite. There should be a greater accent on continued training both for the young and for adults. It should be permissible for a clergyman to admit baptised persons to communion after proper preparation. First communion should where possible be administered by the bishop. Confirmation should continue as a service of commitment and commissioning at a suitable age in adult life. It would be administered either by the bishop or by a priest commissioned by him. It would not be appropriate to confirm a person who has been baptised in adult life. Confirmation should no longer be used as a rite for receiving baptised members of other Churches into the Church of England.

MARRIAGE

The Church of England affirms according to our Lord's teaching 'that marriage is in its nature a union permanent and life-long, for better for worse, till death do them part, of one man with one woman, to the exclusion of all others on either side, for the procreation and nurture of children, for the hallowing and right direction of the natural instincts and affections, and for the mutual society, help, and comfort which the one ought to have of the other, both in prosperity and adversity.'

This affirmation is contained in Canon B.30, which goes on to require the minister to explain the Church's belief to those who apply to him to be married and the need of God's grace to discharge their obligations aright.

No one may be married if they are under sixteen or within the prohibited degrees of kinship. There are also special requirements as to consent for those under eighteen. The position of the unbaptised is not entirely clear. If neither party is baptised marriage in church is probably inappropriate and if one party is not baptised it is desirable to obtain the bishop's directions. Ordinarily a clergyman must marry a resident parishioner, except that he is not required to do so if one of the parties has been in a divorce case and the former spouse is still living. (Canons B.31 and B.32).

Marriage may be celebrated after banns, with a common or special licence or with a superintendent registrar's certificate.

Banns are read in the parish or parishes of residence of the parties and may in addition be read in the parish where one is on the church electoral roll. Bans may be read and marriages celebrated in a daughter church if it is licensed for marriages. Sometimes for special reasons if there is no adequate church there is a right of marriage in an adjoining parish. The names used should be the names by which the persons are generally known. A layman taking morning or evening prayer under the authority of the bishop may read banns.

A common licence is given by an appropriate official under the authority of the bishop or the Archbishop of Canterbury. Marriage must take place in a parish where a party has resided for at least fifteen days. A special licence from the Archbishop of Canterbury can authorise a marriage in any place at any time. An affidavit has to be sworn before a licence is given.

A marriage should usually be solemnised by a priest, but a deacon can do so. Except under a special licence it must be celebrated between eight in the morning and six at night. There should be at least two persons present besides the parties and the minister to act as witnesses.

This is only a brief outline of the law of marriage. The Marriage Act 1949 is the main source and a *résumé* of certain parts is given in Canons B.30 to B.35.

Where persons have contracted a civil marriage Canon B.36 authorises a subsequent service of solemnisation of matrimony. As this is not properly a marriage service the formalities for such a service are unnecessary.

A Report entitled 'Marriage, Divorce and the Church' published in 1971 faced the Synod with the question whether in suitable cases a person whose former marriage has ended in divorce might be remarried in church. While the Report affirmed the rightness of the Church's concept of marriage, it suggested that there need be no complete bar to such remarriage if there was a consensus in the Church that such a bar was not appropriate in the circumstances of today. There was disquiet in the Synod when the Report was first debated and there was no clear reference to dioceses asking for their views. The proposal was considered again in 1973 and there was a clear majority in the Synod against it. On the other hand a proposal to refer the question to the dioceses before a decision was taken was only defeated because there was a tie in the House of Clergy. There is now a considerable likelihood that diocesan synods will discuss the Report, which would lead to a reopening of the issue in the General Synod if the dioceses were not satisfied with the decision taken.

The State's Law Commission in 1973 reported to Parliament on the Solemnisation of Marriage. The main proposals were that there should be uniform civil preliminaries for all marriages regardless of where they are celebrated and that the law relating to publication of banns and common licences should be repealed. The Church could retain banns for the purposes of its own procedures if it needed. The Church authorities have indicated that they see objections to these proposals. It is not known whether legislation will be introduced and if so what its effect will be.

BURIAL AND FUNERALS

If a parishioner dies whether within the parish or not a burial service in the church may be required and also burial of the body or ashes if the parish has a burial ground which is not closed. Any person dying in the parish has the same rights. The ordinary burial service is not supposed to be read over an unbaptised person, a suicide of sound mind or a person who has been excommunicated and was unrepentant. A special form may be used for suicides. In fact the question of soundness of mind depends to some extent on the policy of the coroner, and clergymen often find it necessary to use their judgement on what is appropriate.

A burial service is normally conducted by a clergyman, but a deaconess may act with the good-will of the persons responsible.

Where a body is to be cremated the burial service may precede, accompany or follow the cremation and may be held either in church or at the crematorium. Unless there is a good reason to the contrary ashes should be committed to consecrated ground by a clergyman (Canon B.38).

As cremation is becoming more common the new services are called funeral services rather than burial services.

KEEPING ORDER IN CHURCH

Churchwardens are to ' maintain order and decency in the church and churchyard especially during the time of divine service ' (Canon E.1). It is the duty of the sidesmen to assist them (Canon E.2). Canon F.15 provides that the churchwardens and their assistants are to restrain anyone who behaves riotously, violently or indecently in a church or churchyard whether or not a service is in process, or who troubles or misuses a clergyman taking a service, and if necessary they must proceed against such a person under the law. Should such proceedings seem possibly appropriate a lawyer should be consulted. It is obviously desirable to proceed with care unless the case is a clear one. Certain kinds of behaviour may be irritating without being riotous, violent or indecent or a sufficient nuisance to the clergyman.

SEATING IN CHURCH

Generally speaking the churchwardens assisted by the sidesmen allocate seats at services in the main body of the church and the minister in the chancel. Occasionally individuals have special rights to seats (Canon F.7).

REGISTERS

Under the general law there must be registers of baptism, banns of marriage and marriage, and if there is a burial ground also of burials. Under Canon Law there must be a register of confirmations, and also a register of services in every church used for worship. These registers are provided at the expense of the parochial church council (Canons B.39, F.11 and F.12).

Old registers are often deposited in county record offices or similar places. The consent of a parochial church council is normally required for this to be done. When registers are in the possession of the incumbent they may be searched, and fees or other payments for expenses may be chargeable. (Parochial Registers and Records Measure 1929, Parochial Fees Order 1972.)

11. Pastoral Care

The incumbent has the cure of souls in the parish and something about this subject has already been written in Chapter 3. He has the responsibility for all persons resident in his parish who have not chosen to give their spiritual allegiance elsewhere and all those living elsewhere whose names are on the roll of his parish. Obviously besides his special duties a clergyman would wish also to help anyone who came to him. Sometimes a clergyman who is a stranger can give more help than a person's parish priest.

There are some persons for whom he has a particular care. He is to instruct the children or cause them to be instructed in the Christian faith and use such opportunities of teaching or visiting in the schools within his cure as are open to him. He is to be diligent in visiting his parishioners, particularly those that are sick and infirm. In his care for the sick and those in danger of death he has a special duty to bring them communion and if they so desire he administers the service of laying on of hands. He is to provide opportunity for his parishioners to come to him for counsel and advice. He has a special care for those burdened with a sense of sin (which should be all of us if we have a realistic vision of life). Some such persons may wish to come to him to ' receive the benefit of absolution, together with ghostly counsel and advice to the quieting of his conscience and avoiding of all scruple and doubtfulness '.

A sick person in particular may wish to make a special confession of his sins. (Canons B.28, B.29, B.37 and C.24).

In his pastoral cure he is assisted by any curate that he may have, and his lay people, especially those with any office. He should also seek the co-operation of the parochial church council and indeed of all his lay people as appropriate. In team ministries, as has been indicated in Chapter 3, a rector and vicars share the cure of souls.

THE LAITY
It is the special work of a deaconess ' to exercise pastoral care to instruct the people in the Christian faith and to prepare them

93

for the reception of the sacraments '. (Canon D.1.) The special duties of a woman worker depend on her licence, but might well be phrased in much the same terms. She might have a particular qualification for example as a moral welfare worker (Canon E.7).

A reader's tasks could be ' to visit the sick, to read and pray with them, to teach in Sunday school and elsewhere, and generally to undertake such pastoral and educational work and to give such assistance to any minister as the bishop may direct ' (Canon E.4).

As has already been said in Chapter 3 it is a complete mistake to regard the churchwardens, sidesmen and parochial church council as concerned exclusively or mainly with finance and administration. They also have a general concern for the whole Christian life of the parish including its pastoral and missionary aspects. The law is generally speaking silent on the pastoral duty of lay Christians. Parents and guardians have however their special duty to ensure that their children receive proper instruction (Canon B.26).

But the fundamental truth of pastoral care is that it is the concern of the whole congregation, clergy and laity alike. Each must contribute as he can either with special skills or the ordinary kindness of the good neighbour.

12. The Layman's Life

In earlier centuries it was regarded as right to bind the layman by clear legal duties of church attendance and moral behaviour. Failure to carry these out involved penalties in the civil or ecclesiastical courts. There is now no question of imposed duties beyond those required by the secular law. Obviously certain qualifications are necessary for receiving certain of the ministrations of the Church or for holding certain offices. Equally certain kinds of behaviour may involve disqualifications, for instance refusal of Holy Communion. The question of appropriate disqualifications for lay office holders has been raised, but is not likely to receive early consideration.

The Canon Law does however lay down certain rules for the lay members of the Church which are matters of exhortation not legal requirement.

Sunday is to be celebrated ' as a weekly memorial of our Lord's resurrection and kept according to God's holy will and pleasure, particularly by attendance at divine service, by deeds of charity, and by abstention from all unnecessary labour and business '. Feast days specified in the Prayer Book are to be observed, particularly Christmas, Epiphany, the Annunciation, Easter, Ascension Day, Whitsunday, Trinity Sunday and All Saints' Day. Days of fasting or abstinence and vigils of saints days as set out in the Prayer Book should be observed, particularly Lent and in Lent particularly Ash Wednesday and Holy Week. Good Friday should be observed by prayer and meditation on the passion, by self-discipline and by attendance at divine service (Canon B.6).

The members of the congregation should be reverent and attentive at church and obey the directions of the Prayer Book (Canon B.9).

Those who have been confirmed should receive Holy Communion regularly especially at Christmas, Easter and Whitsun. They should prepare themselves as required by the Prayer Book. (Canon B.15).

Parents or guardians of baptised infants have the same responsibilities as are required of godparents at the baptism service (Canon B.22). They must ensure that their children are instructed in the Christian faith (Canon B.26).

It is the duty of all baptised persons to examine their lives and conversations by the rule of God's commandments and to confess their sins with full purpose of amendment so that they may receive forgiveness. The general confessions and absolutions are to be used for this purpose. If further comfort or counsel is required a person may go to a clergyman as indicated in the preceding chapter (Canon B.29).

There is no obligation for a person to enter his name on the roll of his parish, though practising church members should do so. There is certainly no obligation of office holding. These are tasks which should be undertaken by some, just as there are many other tasks in a parish which require to be done. Every Christian has the obligation to use his time rightly. The layman usually has his own work, his own personal commitments and need for leisure. Over and above that he usually has time to give and capacities to use, and his parish has claims upon these, which he ought to consider. There are also other activities for the good of the community which are Christian work. Everyone must make his own decisions by the light of his own conscience asking for such advice as he thinks fit. There can be no question of binding rules.

Every aspect of the life of man is the concern of God and the Church, and to confine the Christian life to going to services and doing little jobs for the parish is a complete misunderstanding. But the work of the parish needs to be done and well done.

The Church has its own moral and spiritual teaching, but these are not enforced by law. It is for each person to obey or not as his conscience directs him. Some have responsibility for others as well as themselves, parents, employers, shop stewards, teachers. They have to lead others to right living by example and guidance. Compulsion is usually of little use and often harmful.

Around 1950 there was a considerable discussion of the duties of Church membership and the following ' Short Guide to the Duties of Church Membership ' was issued by the Archbishops at the request of the Church Assembly:—

> ' All baptized and confirmed members of the Church must play their full part in its life and witness. That you may fulfil this duty, we call upon you:

To follow the example of Christ in home and daily life, and to bear personal witness to him.

To be regular in private prayer day by day.

To read the Bible carefully.

To come to church every Sunday.

To receive the Holy Communion faithfully and regularly.

To give personal service to church, neighbours, and community.

To give money for the work of parish and diocese and for the work of the Church at home and overseas.

To uphold the standard of marriage entrusted by Christ to his Church.

To care that children are brought up to love and serve the Lord.'

There may well be some who regard the law in this field and the Guide also as unduly ' churchy ' for this day and age. Two comments can perhaps briefly be made. First, the Church's law only operates in its own sphere. Religious observance can to some extent be covered. Missionary or social work to the community cannot be expressed legally except in the most general terms, such as the parochial church council's duty to promote ' in the parish the whole mission of the Church, pastoral, evangelistic, social and ecumenical '. Secondly, while the life of the parish should be lived in love, it should also have a basis in law. The law and the Guide do in fact follow the Gospel in affirming the double duty of love of God and love of one's neighbour, but laying primary emphasis on love of God as expressed in worship and conformity to the life of the Church. To give priority to conformity with the life of society is not the teaching of the Gospel, nor is it the teaching of the law of the Church. Harmony between the two in this country is usually possible and desirable, but the first essential is for the community of the Church and the individual Christian to be in relationship with God. Only in so far as this is true can love and help be really effective in the parish and in the face of the appalling needs of the world. It is also true that the Church must be sensitive to social changes, or society will not listen to the Church. The social teaching of the Church is rightly subject to continued scrutiny and where appropriate modification, and that affects the way the layman governs his life.

13.   Support of the Clergy

The clergy are in a special sense the representatives of the Church in the place where they work and this is true most of all of the incumbent whose office is identified with his parish.   Certain tasks they must or should perform, but the Church in the place is the clergy and laity together as a single whole.   If the clergy are not supported by the laity, only in very limited ways can the work of the Church be done and the lot of the clergy is arduous and depressing.   It is of course also true that the clergy can fail their laity.

The best support of the clergy is for the laity to play their part in the life of the parish with energy and understanding, This includes participating in services and promoting or assisting other activities.   The Church in a place is a family and joining in the life of the family is good in itself, whether or not any further demonstrable result is achieved or intended.   If there is a real life it will strengthen the individual work and witness of clergy and laity.   If there is not, the clergy most of all are likely to suffer in effectiveness and happiness.

Then there is personal friendship.   It is needed and valued anyway, but especially if it is understanding friendship.   Clergymen are ordinary human beings placed in a special position with its special rewards and hardships.   A layman cannot know quite what these are, but he can use his sympathy and imagination and allow a relationship to grow which will be an enrichment to both. This is especially true if a layman realises that he needs help in understanding and living the Christian life, and that the clergyman has experience that he can share with him.   If the relationship does not go beyond ordinary friendship then there is failure.

And of course the clergyman is especially vulnerable.   Just as the Church suffers from wild attacks based on lack of understanding and hostility (as well as profiting from useful and kindly criticism) so also there can be suffering for the clergyman if his actions and words are distorted or things are expected of him which are outside his functions or beyond his powers, perhaps because of lack of support from his laity.

Incumbents are office holders and in the past it was expected of them that they should live from the stipend attached to their office. They were expected not to need to rely either on the diocese or on their parishioners for at least the necessities of life. Therefore they could carry out their duties without fear or favour.

A major source of income used to be tithes, a tenth part of the crops and animals produced on land in the parish which was not exempt. Tithes became commuted into money payments called tithe rent-charges and these rent-charges have now been extinguished.

Benefices have their endowments. These may consist of land or houses, called glebe, which may be used for church purposes, but if not so used are sources of financial profit to the incumbent through letting. This can be substantial and indeed a benefice occasionally greatly increases in value through some fortunate accident such as the discovery of minerals or urban development in districts which were previously agricultural. Acting as land-lord can however be an embarrassing situation for a clergyman and few have a real knowledge of or interest in property matters. Many dioceses manage glebe on behalf of the incumbents. The acreage of glebe is falling as there is a tendency to sell it. In 1972 the General Synod decided that all benefice endowment income should be pooled and that glebe should be transferred into dio-cesan ownership. The necessary legislation to achieve this is expected to be introduced in 1974, but it will be a few years before it can be passed and brought into full effect.

The Church Commissioners, the bishop and the patron are interested parties in buying, selling or leasing glebe, but parochial church councils are not legally involved unless they are affected in particular ways, for example if they except liability for the rent or repair of a glebe house which is to be a residence for a curate or other parochial officer. The cost of repairs is normally met out of benefice income.

The endowments of benefices in the form of investments used to be held by the Church Commissioners as separate funds. In 1951 by the Benefices (Stabilization of Incomes) Measure these endowments were transferred to the general fund of the Church Commissioners and an appropriate income paid. This avoids fluctuations of income. Benefice income may also be received from trust funds not held by the Church Commissioners.

If a benefice is excessively rich, part of the endowment can be transferred for the general benefit of the clergy in the diocese but normally this requires the consent of the incumbent except at a vacancy. When benefice income is pooled the task of dividing it fairly will become easier.

In 1972 the Synod appointed the Church Commissioners as the Central Stipends Authority and gave them power to co-ordinate the work of the dioceses.

Usually the incumbent has a customary right to the offerings on Easter Sunday, but sometimes the parochial church council makes other arrangements particularly where systems of stewardship affect the collection of offerings at services.

The incumbent receives fees for marriages and burials and for permitting the erection of monuments in the churchyard. Certain fees are fixed by Acts of Parliament and others by a table of fees fixed and revised when appropriate by the Church Commissioners under the Ecclesiastical Fees Measure 1962. The present table was fixed in 1972. Fees are also paid to the person doing the work of the parish clerk (often the incumbent) or the sexton and the parochial church council also receives fees for a marriage or burial service, for a burial and for the erection of a monument.

An assistant curate's stipend must be agreed when he is appointed. It used normally to be paid out of the benefice income.

The income which most clergymen receive as of right is in these days inadequate and has to be made up to a reasonable figure.

In this connection it should be remembered that there are limits to the occupations in which a clergyman is entitled to engage if he is exercising his orders. He is for example allowed to be a schoolmaster or to farm his glebe subject to certain restrictions but is prohibited from engaging in most kinds of trade or business. By Canon C.28 of the new code of Canons however the bishop may give him a licence to engage in trading or other occupations provided he is satisfied that the proper performance of his duties would not be affected. Before reaching a decision on whether or not to grant a licence the bishop must consult the parochial church council. A licence may be given not for the purpose of increasing the income of the clergy but to enable him to engage in work which will bring him into contact with others engaged on the same work on equal terms. In other words, the motive should be evangelistic and not financial at all.

HOUSING

In most parishes there is a parsonage house in which the incumbent must reside unless he has a licence not to do so. He must not be absent for more than three months in the year without a licence. If there is no parsonage house the bishop may allow him to reside in some other suitable house (Canon C.25).

The parsonage house is usually owned by the incumbent and there is no proposal to change this situation. Under the Repair of Benefice Buildings Measure 1972 the house is inspected every five years and the repairs are then carried out and financed by the diocesan parsonages board. Money is obtained partly from grants by the Commissioners and partly from contributions from the parochial church council, fixed in a manner laid down by a diocesan scheme. This system covers only repairs, not improvements or interior decorations.

The building, purchasing, selling or major improvement of a parsonage house is governed by the Parsonages Measure, 1938. The incumbent (or the bishop during a vacancy) executes the necessary instruments, but the consent of the Church Commissioners, the bishop and the diocesan parsonages board are required. The patron and the parochial church council must be consulted. The profits or liabilities on these transactions at law fall on the benefice.

EXPENSES OF THE CLERGY

The incumbent is expected at law to meet his expenses of office, postage, telephone, office expenses, the provision and running of a car, travelling expenses, entertainment. It is highly desirable unless it is quite impracticable that the parochial church council should meet these commitments. It is not fair that incumbents should pay them from their stipends which are often limited, and unless they are very self-sacrificing there is a natural temptation to economise beyond what the circumstances really require.

SUPPORT BY THE CHURCH COMMISSIONERS

The Church Commissioners manage considerable funds, which passed into their hands from their two predecessors, Queen Anne's Bounty and the Ecclesiastical Commissioners, and represent the historic endowments of the Church. These funds are used almost entirely for the improvement of the living conditions of the clergy. Part is earmarked for particular benefices or other special objects, and the surplus is allocated mainly in block grants to dioceses for the stipends and housing of the clergy.

In addition the Commissioners pay pensions to clergymen on their retirement either because of age or infirmity and to their widows and dependants. No contribution is required for these pensions from the clergyman or from any other source.

Although the Commissioner's income is considerable the needs of the Church are also considerable and there is no question of there being spare money. It is rather a question of deciding which claims upon it are most compelling. By law it is only available for certain specified purposes, which do not include the improvement or repair of church buildings, the payment of lay people who do not assist in the cure of souls, training for the ministry, diocesan quotas, overseas missions or the relief of the needy here and abroad.

SUPPORT BY THE DIOCESE AND PARISH

It is the duty of the diocesan authorities to ensure that the clergy who hold benefices or are licensed to work in the diocese are properly paid and housed, and appropriate stipends are fixed by the diocesan authorities in the light of the policy agreed by the synod and of advice (and where appropriate directions) by the Central Stipends Authority. Targets are fixed centrally, but there are variations between dioceses both in their methods of calculation and the levels reached. Each diocese by law must have a diocesan stipends fund which is held by the Church Commissioners and into which are paid the block grants from the Commissioners for stipends. The diocese may also have some funds of its own, but the balance required must be found from the laity, probably through quotas from parishes.

The diocesan authorities also have a programme for the improvement and replacement of parsonage houses using money provided by the Commissioners and other sums raised by themselves. They also ensure that no incumbent has to meet personally the cost of the rent, rates or repair of his parsonage house. Many dioceses have schemes to assist over interior decorations of parsonages or over other houses occupied by clergy.

The situation therefore is that there is money available for the payment and housing of the clergy, but this is not nearly sufficient without contributions from the laity. How these contributions should be made depends not on law but on policy which may change continually. Therefore it is not appropriate for this book to go too deeply into these important questions. One factor in deciding policy is to gain maximum benefit from the law relating to income tax and kindred subjects.

It should also be emphasised that the Church's lay workers require support and assistance as well as the clergy and if there are such workers in any parish they are the responsibility of that parish. All paid parochial lay workers are the responsibility to some extent of the diocese and therefore of all the parishes within the diocese.

14. A New Incumbent

Where there is a vacancy through the resignation or death or removal of an incumbent the parochial church council must be notified. The patron is responsible for finding a new incumbent, but obviously the parish has an interest. What can be done is set out in the Benefices (Exercise of Rights of Presentation) Measure 1931. The parochial church council may make written representations to the patron on the conditions, needs and traditions of the parish, but they should not mention the name of any particular clergyman. A copy of the letter to the patron must be sent to the bishop.

Besides writing this letter the council can also within thirty days of notification of the vacancy pass a resolution requiring that consultation should take place with the patron as provided in the Measure. The patron must then consult the churchwardens about the clergyman he wishes to present to the bishop and may present if the churchwardens' consent. If the churchwardens do not consent or if they do not meet the patron although he offers a meeting the patron can apply to the bishop after sixty days from notification of the vacancy. The patron or the parochial church council can require the bishop to consult a diocesan committee called the body of advisers before reaching a decision or the bishop may consult them of his own accord. The bishop can then accept the presentation or refuse it on the grounds that the clergyman is unsuitable. If he refuses the patron can appeal to the archbishop.

The bishop may of his own accord refuse to institute a clergyman presented to him if he was ordained deacon less than three years ago, or because of insufficient learning, physical or mental infirmity, serious pecuniary embarrassment, grave misconduct or neglect of duty in carrying out a previous office, evil life or having caused scandal since his ordination, or in the case of a person who has not been an incumbent or vicar in a team ministry if he has not had three years parochial experience, or if there was some kind of illegal bargain over the presentation (Canon C.10).

If the bishop is himself the patron which is quite often the case there is no presentation or institution, but instead the bishop collates, which produces the same results. The provisions of the Benefices (Exercise of Rights of Presentation) Measure apply with necessary modifications.

INSTITUTION AND INDUCTION

When a presentation is accepted by the bishop he gives at least one month's notice of his intention to institute to the church-wardens and they must at once put the notice from the bishop on the door of the principal church of the parish. At the end of the month they return it to the bishop with a certificate that it has been exhibited (Benefices Act 1898, section 2, Benefices Rules 1926).

Institution admits a clergyman to the cure of souls and spiritual duties of the benefice. Induction admits a clergyman to the property rights of the benefice.

Institution is performed by the diocesan bishop or another bishop authorised by him. As a last resort a clergyman other than the bishop can be authorised to institute. Institution almost invariably takes place at a service in the parish church, though this is not essential. The bishop reads the words of institution from a written instrument with the bishop's seal attached. The clergyman meanwhile kneels and holds the seal. Before institution he must make a declaration of assent to the Thirty-nine Articles and the Book of Common Prayer, a declaration against simony and take the oaths of allegiance to the Crown and canonical obedience to the bishop (Canons C.10 and C.13 to C.16). A new form of the declaration of assent has been approved by the Synod but is not yet in use. It will be found on page 11.

Induction is carried out by the archdeacon on the orders of the bishop or by a deputy, often the rural dean. The person induct-ing takes the clergyman by the hand and lays it on the key or the ring of the church door while he speaks the words of induction. He then opens the door and admits the clergyman into the church and the clergyman tolls the bell to announce the induction (Canon C.11).

Shortly after institution and induction, probably on the first Sunday, the new incumbent is required publicly to read the Thirty-nine Articles, but this will not be neccessary when the new Canon on the declaration of assent comes into operation.

15. A Vacancy

When a vacancy occurs in a benefice the work of the Church must go on. If there is a staff of curates there may be little difficulty. Occasionally a clergyman is licensed by the bishop to take charge of the parish, in which case as far as services and pastoral care are concerned he is virtually in the position of the incumbent. He also acts as chairman of the parochial church council. But if there is no priest licensed to the charge of the parish the chair is taken by the lay vice-chairman. There is a special kind of vacancy where the right of presentation is suspended so that the vacancy is bound to continue. A clergyman, perhaps the incumbent of a neighbouring parish, is often licensed as priest in charge. He also acts as chairman of the parochial church council. Suspension of presentation will be discussed briefly in the chapter on Pastoral Reorganisation.

SEQUESTRATORS

When there is a vacancy sequestrators are appointed by the bishop and act on his behalf. Usually they are the churchwardens and the rural dean. The appointment is made by a writ issued by the diocesan registrar who also provides a copy. The writ is placed on the door of the church for the first Sunday. The certificate upon it is then signed by one of the sequestrators and sent to the Church Commissioners so that they can register the writ and know that they must deal with the sequestrators over benefice income and liabilities. The copy of the writ is placed on the church notice board.

It is the duty of the sequestrators to ensure that services are held and if necessary that payments are made to those taking services, which payments should cover the appropriate fee and expenses. The rural dean is usually the person who assists over arrangements beyond those possible within the resources of the parish. Appropriate fees for clergymen and lay workers are laid down by the bishop.

The sequestrators collect benefice income from the Church Commissioners and possibly grants from the diocesan stipends funds according to whether such grants are made and if so on what terms. They may cease in whole or in part during the vacancy. The sequestrators also receive glebe income and fees which would ordinarily go to the incumbent, though these are often paid to the person carrying out the duty. They have no claim on the Easter offerings which are treated like collections on any ordinary Sunday.

The sequestrators pay the stipend of any clergyman taking over the parish, and if there is an assistant curate who has extra responsibilities because of the vacancy the bishop can permit them to pay him an additional remuneration. The cost of visiting preachers must also be met. Sequestrators supervise the parsonage house and pay outgoings including any necessary repairs, but no work should be put in hand except on the orders of the parsonages board. They should make proper provision for the upkeep of the parsonage garden but should not engage a full-time gardener without authority. If an incumbent dies his widow is entitled to remain in the parsonage house for two months. There may be expenses in connection with glebe. Any changes in lettings of glebe are a matter for the bishop not the sequestrators. The bishop also takes the initiative over sales or purchases of parsonage houses and glebe.

Careful accounts must be kept and every effort must be made not to exceed the benefice income, as the new incumbent is liable for a debit balance. He also receives any credit balance and this can be a great help to him at a time when he inevitably has extra expenses.

This account of the duties of sequestrators is a brief one because the law is so complex. Few lay people are involved in it and when they are there are those with knowledge to advise them. *Notes for Sequestrators* prepared by the Legal Advisory Commission of the General Synod are obtainable from the Church House Bookshop, price 11p.

16. Buildings for Worship

Almost nothing has been written as yet about the church buildings, for many people the obvious reminder of the existence of the Church and the Christian faith. The traditional idea is that of a prominent building set in a convenient position at which a large part of the community attends worship on a Sunday. The realities of modern life particularly in the great urban areas often bear not the remotest resemblance to this traditional picture and there is considerable discussion about the right kind of provision of buildings for worship, ranging from the view just described to the view that the Church has in many situations no need of special buildings at all. The law is now much more flexible, and experiments can be conducted to discover what is the best answer in the various situations that arise today.

In the last years of the Church Assembly a Commission was considering the execution and financing of repairs to church buildings. The General Synod established a new permanent body under its own auspices called the Council for Places of Worship and entrusted to it the task of considering not only repairs to churches but the law relating the church buildings generally. There are also working parties on the Pastoral Measure 1968 and State Aid for Churches. The proposals of these three bodies could lead to considerable changes in the law on this subject, but at the present time the work is not sufficiently far advanced for much to be reported.

CONSECRATED, DEDICATED AND LICENSED BUILDINGS

At law a church means a consecrated church, that is a building set apart for ever for sacred purposes. It must be built on freehold land held for the purpose, and the bishop must then be asked to consecrate it. The sentence of consecration is worded in strong terms which suggest that there can be no question of the sacred use being brought to an end or the building ever being used for any secular purpose at all. In fact however the law is much more liberal.

Before the coming into operation of the Pastoral Measure 1968 there could not be a parish unless there was a consecrated church considered by the Church Commissioners to be suitable to be a parish church. Until an area had such a building it remained what was called an ecclesiastical district and did not have the full status of a parish. Now every separate area established by legal scheme must be a parish, and the only areas which are not parishes are conventional districts which depend upon agreements between the bishop and the incumbent or incumbents concerned, which any party can bring to an end at any time.

A parish need not now have a traditional parish church but may have some suitable building licensed for worship instead. There could be a temporary dedicated building or a dual purpose building, part church and part hall. There could be what the Pastoral Measure calls a parish centre of worship, which might consist of a room for services and rooms allocated to meet other social and pastoral needs, and perhaps also residential accommodation for the staff. A parish in a new housing area might use a hall or a large room until the congregation had built up its own life and decided what permanent solution would best meet the needs of the situation.

If a building is designated a parish centre of worship then it is treated as a parish church for all purposes except that a parishioner who is being married has the option of going to a neighbouring parish with a ' proper ' church if he or she prefers. Where there is no church building licensed for marriages this use of a neighbouring parish church is necessary anyway.

There can be more than one building used for worship in a parish and these buildings can be consecrated, dedicated or only licensed for worship. Church buildings which are not the parish church are called chapels of ease, but the term daughter church is more commonly used. If there are two consecrated churches one can be substituted for the other as the parish church. Another new possibility permitted by the Pastoral Measure is that there can be two parish churches in a parish. This might be particularly appropriate where two communities with churches of a similar size are joined as one parish (Sections 27 and 29 of the Pastoral Measure 1968).

SHARED BUILDINGS

It is also possible for a building for worship to be shared by two or more Churches under the Sharing of Church Buildings Act 1969. This can be an existing building belonging to one of the Churches, or a new building erected for the purpose, probably in a new housing area. The Act applies to the Church of England, the Roman Catholic Church and the major Nonconformist Churches. The Churches enter into a sharing agreement and on the Church of England side the parties would be the incumbent, the parochial church council and the diocesan board of finance. The consent of the bishop and the pastoral committee would also be required.

The buildings to be shared could be the parish church or parish centre of worship, other church buildings, halls or residence houses. A sharing agreement might involve the joint ownership of a building as well as the shared use. In such a case the building would be managed by trustees instead of by the ordinary Church authorities. The agreement would regulate the nature and times of services and any joint participation in conducting services, and also the management and financial obligations of administering and if necessary providing the building. Problems over solemnising marriages would have to be resolved. There must be power to amend the sharing agreement and if necessary to bring it to an end.

A number of complicated issues are likely to arise and parishes which plan to have a shared building will need to seek advice and help. The Act will also need to be kept under scrutiny to ensure that it adequately reflects the developing ecumenical situation.

OWNERSHIP AND MAINTENANCE OF CHURCHES

Usually the incumbent is the owner of the church, but in practice ownership means little. The incumbent has the general control of the building subject to the rights of others. He cannot make any substantial alteration in it or dispose of it on his own authority. Sometimes the ownership rests with a rector who is not the incumbent. Such a rector may be a clergyman or a lay person or a cathedral chapter or college or some other corporate body. Churches are also sometimes owned by trustees.

The usual arrangement for repairing church buildings was that the chancel was the responsibility of the rector and that the remainder of the church was the responsibility of the parishioners. Clerical rectors no longer have this liability but it still sometimes rests with a layman or a corporate body. Before 1868 a rate could be levied for the repair of the church, and this was the usual practice unless rich parishioners provided the money. Between 1868 and 1921 the churchwardens had to raise the money from such sources as were available. In 1921 this duty was transferred to the parochial church council by the Parochial Church Councils (Powers) Measure of that year. The relevant section is now section 4 of the Parochial Church (Powers) Measure 1956.

The Inspection of Churches Measure 1955 requires every church to be inspected by an architect chosen by the parochial church council and approved as suitable by the diocesan advisory committee for the care of churches. The architect reports to the parochial church council and the archdeacon. His fees are met by that council unless other provision is made by the diocese. If no arrangements for an inspection are made within five years from the last inspection the archdeacon may require the parochial church council to take action and if they do not do so the archdeacon may order an inspection himself.

There is no machinery to ensure that the repairs indicated in the report are carried out, but Canon F.18 requires the archdeacon or the rural dean to survey churches every three years and an important feature of these surveys is to ensure that inspections are made and repairs carried out. The annual visitation is also an obvious occasion for enquiry.

Canon F.13 requires that churches be kept in proper repair and there is a special provision for the keeping of records for every church and chapel in the parish of alterations, additions, removals and repairs. The record for each church must be kept in a book provided for the purpose, which must state where specifications and plans may be inspected if not deposited with the book.

Repairs to church buildings, particularly ancient buildings, can be extremely expensive and parishes sometimes have great difficulty in finding the money. Some dioceses give a certain amount of help and there are a number of trusts which provide money for the repair either of churches or of historic buildings generally. Local authorities have power to contribute under a recent Act. The Church Commissioners have no general power to provide money for the repair of churches, and no Government money is available for churches in use for worship.

Negotiations on the possibility of State aid are taking place between the Department of the Environment and a Synod Working Party. There has been a careful investigation into the situation in specimen dioceses and the Department has shown sympathy with the Church's case.

The repair of the church has always been a particular responsibility of the parish so the incumbent and the churchwardens should ensure that a careful watch is kept and that all appropriate action such as clearing gutters and drain pipes is taken. In this way damage may be avoided and any repairs that are necessary can be undertaken quickly and at less cost.

THE AUTHORISATION OF ALTERATIONS

A church is not regarded as the possession of the parish entirely at the disposal of the parish authorities. It is also under the care of the diocese and no alteration or repair of substance may be carried out either to the fabric or contents of the church without proper authority. Small matters such as replacements of panes of glass or buying new hassocks do not require such authority.

The faculty jurisdiction only became fully formulated in the last century partly as a result of the ritual controversies of that time and the control at law over alterations of substance is now recognised as complete. If the parish authorities decide to alter or repair their church or introduce or remove a fitting or ornament an application must be made to the diocesan registrar. The right persons to apply on behalf of the parish are the incumbent and churchwardens. Any person can however apply, but an application is not likely to be successful unless it has the support of the parish authorities.

There are now two methods of authorisation. If an application is made by the incumbent and churchwardens backed by a resolution of the parochial church council and relates to repair or redecoration, then the authority of the archdeacon is sufficient. Repairs to the church must not involve substantial change in the structure of the building nor affect its appearance either externally or internally and repairs to the contents must not materially affect the nature or appearance of the objects. The archdeacon may also authorise an alteration in an existing heating system which does not involve a substantial change in the appearance of the church either externally or internally. Otherwise a faculty from the chancellor acting on behalf of the bishop is necessary, unless the chancellor allows the matter to be referred to the archdeacon because he believes it is unlikely to give rise to controversy or dissatisfaction and is not of sufficient importance to justify the expense of proceedings for a faculty.

The jurisdiction applies to all consecrated churches and any other building licensed for worship which the bishop orders to be brought under the jurisdiction.

If application is made for an archdeacon's certificate the incumbent and churchwardens must apply on the correct form and certify that notice of the application has been given in the parish. The notice must be on the door of the parish church and the church to which the application relates if it is not the parish church for not less than ten days including two Sundays. If there is any objection then a certificate cannot be given. The application must come before the diocesan advisory committee for the care of churches, which consists of the archdeacons and other persons appointed by the bishop, and the archdeacon cannot grant a certificate unless the committee consents. It is desirable in practice to consult the advisory committee at an early stage. If a certificate cannot be granted or is refused by the archdeacon a petition can still be made for a faculty.

If a faculty is sought then the petition is sent to the registrar and shown to the chancellor who directs that a notice should be placed on the church door as just described for the application for an archdeacon's certificate. If there is no objection and the chancellor thinks fit he can grant a faculty. If there is an objection or the chancellor is not satisfied then there must be a hearing. Hearings are not usual and it seems unnecessary to go into the complicatd law involved. Fees are charged for both faculties and archdeacons' certificates.

A faculty is not necessary for the building of a church. It can permit the demolition of a church but only if another church is to be built or if the building is a dangerous structure. Partial demolition by faculty is possible provided the remaining part is to continue to be used for public worship. There are special provisions about notice and procedure in these cases. In other cases where a church is to be demolished because it is no longer required a faculty is not appropriate but the procedure under the Pastoral Measure must be used. This is described later in this chapter and in chapter 19.

For works of any substance on the external fabric of a church building it is usually necessary to approach the local planning authority as well.

Faculties are also required for the sale of books and valuables not exhibited in the church.

(See the Faculty Jurisdiction Measure 1964 and the Faculty Jurisdiction Rules 1967.)

CHURCHES NO LONGER REQUIRED

If a church is no longer required for worship then it can be declared redundant by a scheme made under the Pastoral Measure 1968. If it is a case of replacing one building by another and the redundant church is of no historic value it can be demolished at once. If a suitable use has already been agreed the scheme can authorise that use. On a declaration of redundancy the church passes out of the care of the parish authorities into that of the diocesan board of finance.

There is then a waiting period of between one and three years during which every effort is made to find a use for the building. It may be another spiritual use such as the chapel of a university or other institution or the church of another denomination. It could be used for other Church purposes such as a hall or being divided into offices. It could be sold or otherwise assigned for suitable secular uses. If no use can be found and the building is of historic or artistic importance it could be maintained by the Redundant Churches Fund. This Fund was established by the Pastoral Measure for this purpose. Money is provided by the Government, the Church Commissioners and from part of the

115

proceeds of sale of redundant church buildings and sites up to £100,000 in five years. Expenditure in the first five years is expected to approach £500,000 and in the second £1,750,000. The Government is willing to provide £700,000 towards the latter sum if the Church provides the rest. This is not a large sum in view of the cost of maintaining ancient buildings. If no use can be found for a redundant church and it is not transferred to the Fund it must be demolished and the site disposed of. The remainder of the proceeds of sale beyond that allocated to the Redundant Churches Fund goes to the diocesan pastoral accounts which are used primarily for new churches and other buildings required in new housing areas.

(See the Pastoral Measure 1968, sections 28, 29 and 42–66.)

THE CONTENTS OF CHURCHES

By Canon Law a church is required to have a font, a holy table, a pulpit, a lectern, communion plate, communion linen, surplices for the minister, at least one church bell, seats for those attending services, a large Bible including the Apocrypha, a large Prayer Book, a Bible to be kept in the pulpit, a service book with a cushion or desk for the communion table, register books and an alms box. The alms are to be used as agreed between the minister and parochial church council or if they disagree as decided by the bishop. The parochial church council is responsible for ensuring that these necessary articles are provided (Canon F.1–14).

Other articles are also permitted, for instance candlesticks, pictures and crosses. There was a considerable amount of controversy about certain articles during the last century on the ground that they suggested false doctrine or were liable to superstitious use. The law is, in the view of various commissions which have considered it, confusing and out of date. The controversies have died down to a large extent and it does not seem necessary to discuss this subject in detail here.

The goods and ornaments of the church are the property of the churchwardens. They must keep an inventory of these up to date, and must check it with their successors when handing over the goods (Canon E.1, para 5).

The General Synod's Council for Places of Worship presented a report called *Treasures on Earth* to the Synod in 1973. There are problems about the safe-keeping of valuables belonging to the Church and also problems when these valuables are not required for use and the parish is in urgent need of money for important purposes. In suitable cases sales may be permitted by faculty, but a faculty will only be granted after a careful weighing of the issues involved. Parishes with valuables may wish to take advice as to safe-keeping and certainly careful thought would be necessary if a sale were contemplated.

THE USE OF CHURCHES

The sentence of consecration suggests that a church may only be used for Church of England worship. In fact joint services with other Churches and services of other Churches are sometimes conducted. Canon F.15 provides that ' the churchwardens and their assistants shall not suffer the church or chapel to be profaned by any meeting therein for temporal objects inconsistent with the sanctity of the place '.

Canon F.16 relates to plays, concerts and exhibitions of films and pictures in churches. The incumbent must take care that they are ' such as befit the House of God, are consonant with sound doctrine, and make for the edifying of the people '. The bishop may give general directions about this matter and the incumbent should refer cases of doubt to the bishop. The local and other authorities must be consulted about such matters as fire precautions.

In 1973 the Synod considered the question of the use of churches and other church property by other faiths. Where Christian churches are involved there is no reason of general principle why Church of England buildings should not be used by them or transferred to them, though there may be reasons why this is undesirable in a particular case. The Synod decided by a small majority that the use of redundant church buildings by religious bodies which are not Christian was not desirable.

17. Churchyards

Churchyards usually surround the church but there may be separate burial grounds controlled by the parish authorities. Some parishes have no church burial grounds. As with churches ownership is usually in the incumbent, but may be in a rector who is not an incumbent or in trustees. The rights of ownership are extremely limited and the usual one quoted is the right to graze sheep. Presumably such a prospect arouses no more than a mild academic interest in most incumbents.

In 1921 the duty of seeing that the churchyard is maintained was transferred from the churchwardens to the parochial church council. The legal duty only extends to proper fencing and ensuring reasonable access to parishioners making ordinary use of the churchyard, but it is highly desirable that there should be a reasonable standard as an untidy churchyard gives a very bad impression of Church life in the parish.

If a churchyard becomes full and it is no longer appropriate for further burials to take place it can be closed by order in council under the Burial Acts. Orders have in the past been limited to cases where there is a danger to public health. When a churchyard is closed the duty of maintenance may be transferred to the local authority. The Local Government Act 1972 provides a much simpler procedure for a parochial church council to request a local authority to take over the maintenance.

Local authorities are able to contribute to the cost of maintaining churchyards by virtue of the Local Government Act 1972. A churchyard may be transferred to the local authority under the Open Spaces Act 1906.

BUILDING ON CHURCHYARDS AND DISPOSAL OF CHURCHYARDS

Schemes under the Pastoral Measure may permit the whole or part of a churchyard to be used for purposes specified in the scheme or sold. The scheme may permit building in the churchyard provided either there has been no burial in any part affected for fifty years, or, if there has been, no relative or personal representative of a deceased person objects. If human remains would be disturbed, they must be removed. The Measure contains detailed provisions about human remains and monuments. (See Sections 30, 51 and 65.)

GRAVES AND MONUMENTS

While parishioners and others dying in a parish have a right of burial in a churchyard if there is one that has not been closed, this right is confined to burial in a place designated by the incumbent and they have no right to the exclusive use of that place. A grave space can however be reserved by faculty. Such a faculty issued before the passing of the Faculty Jurisdiction Measure 1964 comes to an end in 2064 and since 1964 no faculty may be granted lasting more than 100 years. A further faculty can however be granted to continue the reservation. In practice the erection of a monument serves the same purpose as a reservation.

The faculty jurisdiction extends to consecrated churchyards and the surrounds of a consecrated church whether consecrated or not. A faculty therefore should strictly be required for a monument. In practice an incumbent is permitted to authorise an ordinary kind of monument, but unusual ones should be subject to faculty. In most dioceses the chancellor has made regulations indicating how far the discretion of the incumbent extends.

Monuments when erected belong to those who erected them and their successors, who should carry out any necessary repairs. A faculty can be granted for the removal of a monument unless the owner agrees to move it himself.

18. Visitations

In most years the archdeacon conducts a visitation, but some-times the bishop does so. Visitations are usually held after Easter and churchwardens are admitted at them. Usually a number of parishes are grouped together for a visitation. The purpose of visitations is to enable those responsible for the parishes to know what is happening in them and to correct anything that is going wrong.

When the archdeacon summons the clergy and churchwardens to a visitation he sends articles of enquiry, that is a list of questions about the affairs of the parishes. The clergy and churchwardens frame their presentments which are answers to the articles of enquiry. Presentments can be made on other matters. The archdeacon delivers a charge to those attending the visitation (Canons G.5 and G.6).

For meeting the costs of the visitation each parochial church council pays a small fee.

19. Pastoral Reorganisation

WHAT CAN BE DONE

A number of references have been made to the Pastoral Measure 1968 and the main changes authorised by it described. The Measure contains a new code for pastoral reorganisation. Schemes or orders can be made for a number of purposes, including creating new benefices and parishes or uniting or dividing them or altering their boundaries, creating or bringing to an end team or group ministries, permitting clergymen to hold benefices in plurality, creating archdeaconries or rural deaneries or altering their boundaries or uniting them, designating parish churches, declaring churches redundant and dealing with them, dealing with churchyards and diverting the endowments of a benefice if they are excessive. In carrying out these major objects arrangements have to be made for all kinds of subsidiary matters.

In order to carry out pastoral reorganisation it is often desirable to leave benefices vacant, for example if two benefices are to be combined. The bishop may suspend the patron's right to present for a period not exceeding five years, which may be renewed any number of times. The consent of the diocesan pastoral committee must be obtained and the patron and parochial church council must be consulted. A notice of the suspension is posted on the church door. A suspension can be brought to an end if appropriate, and the patron may then present. If proposals are made for a scheme or order, these sometimes act as a suspension of presentation while the proposals are under consideration.

PROCEDURE

Each diocese has a pastoral committee. The diocesan bishop can be the chairman or a member or neither just as he chooses. The suffragan bishops and archdeacons are members and the board of finance, parsonages board and advisory committee for the care of churches are represented. The remaining members are appointed or elected in such manner as the diocesan synod decides. The committee considers the pastoral organisation of the diocese as required or permitted by the bishop, and makes proposals to him when it believes them to be appropriate. It must pay regard both to the needs of the whole diocese and to the conditions, needs and traditions of individual parishes.

Before any proposals are made by the committee to the bishop all interested parties are consulted. These might be incumbents, team vicars, parochial church councils, patrons, archdeacons, rural deans and the local planning authority. Incumbents, vicars and parochial church councils have the right of meeting the committee or a representative or representatives, and the first two can when their interests are vitally affected insist on seeing the whole committee.

The committee can then formulate definite proposals and put them to the bishop. If he approves he can send them to the Church Commissioners to be embodied in schemes or orders. The Commissioners send the proposals to the interested parties with the information that they will have the right to make representations. A draft scheme or order is then prepared and sent to interested parties. An order is appropriate for less important matters. In the case of a scheme a notice must be posted on the church door. Representations may be sent to the Commissioners within 28 days. Amendments may then be made and if so must be communicated to interested parties so that they can make representations if they wish. If an order is appropriate it can then be made by the bishop on the terms decided by the Commissioners. If a scheme is appropriate it has to be confirmed by an order in council and the interested parties can appeal to the Judicial Committee of the Privy Council.

A simplified procedure is permitted for less important matters if the interested parties are all satisfied. The most usual case is the holding by a clergyman of two or more benefices in plurality. There are additional procedural safeguards if there is a proposal to declare a church redundant, and there is a quite separate procedure for deciding the future of a church after it has been declared redundant.

The Pastoral Measure is long and complex. A description of the provisions of general interest is contained in *A Guide to the Pastoral Measure,* by the author of this book. The Measure is under review by a Working Party.

Conclusion

To revise a book written four years ago makes one conscious of the process of change. Projects which were at the planning stage or not even contemplated are now in operation. New projects are planned. Society changes at an accelerating rate. The Church changes with it. But should it?

Clergymen and laymen alike have their temptations to resist change. The layman in his work, in his ordinary life sees a continuing, often bewildering, movement. Let the Church stay as it was. Let that at least be solid ground. Do not change our services. Do not change our accepted standards. Do not change our buildings. Do not change our organisation.

God does not change. That is certain. But God has willed a changing world, and the Church must be sensitive to its movement. If it loses touch with the world, it may find that God is with the world against the Church.

The synods are organs of change for the Church. That is one reason why they are necessary. That is one reason why they are often unpopular.

Looking to the future it would be wrong to predict the course of change. That is for the Church to decide under the guidance of God as year succeeds to year. But two things perhaps can safely be said.

First, the Church needs to lighten ship. There is too much organisation, too much tradition that is largely drained of meaning, too many buildings. In some ways there is an attraction in such things, but even the attraction is of doubtful value. They can become a refuge from the world, and the world will pass by those that take refuge from it. Life as it is needs to be lived and the Church has to get to grips with it.

Secondly, the changes that happen tend towards unity of the Church. This is found within the Church of England itself. The party argument or party speech carries much less weight than it used to. The Churches also grope towards each other. There are often set-backs because the movement made or the time chosen may not be rightly judged, but all the time the current is flowing. Therefore the Church of England needs to think, not how to retain its individuality, but how to contribute what it has to the whole, and how to receive from the whole what others contribute. As there is the need for the individual to express his own personality so the particular lines of thinking that are found in this and other Churches must have their place. The Church must be comprehensive. Unity can only happen gradually, but the movement towards it cannot be abandoned. There is the divine imperative that the Church must be one.

Bibliography

There is a considerable amount of literature about the matters covered by this book, but this bibliography is confined to official publications and others published by the Church Information Office to assist those at work in parishes. All are obtainable at the Church House Bookshop, Great Smith Street, Westminster, SW1P 3BN.

LEGISLATION

Church Representation Rules.   40p

Church Representation Rules—New Developments 1974.   3p

Synodical Government Measure 1969.   HMSO, 27½p

Pastoral Measure 1968.   HMSO, 68p

A Guide to the Pastoral Measure, by Michael Elliott-Binns.   25p

Benefices (Exercise of Rights of Presentation) Measure 1931.   HMSO, 5p

Church of England (Worship and Doctrine) Measure
(This has not yet received the Royal Assent and the price is not known but copies of a General Synod version are obtainable)

The Canons of the Church of England.   SPCK
(New edition in preparation)

CARE OF CHURCHES SERIES
Published for the Council for Places of Worship by CIO, written by experts and produced in uniform (A4) format.

How to Look After Your Church.   25p

Church Organs.   25p

Sound Amplification in Your Church.   15p

Economical Churchyard Maintenance.   7½p

It Won't Happen to Us.   (A comprehensive guide to church insurance).   25p

Wallpaintings: Questions and Answers.   7½p

Lighting and Wiring of Churches.   40p

Church Wiring.   (Part II of Lighting and Wiring).   20p

Heating your Church. 40p

Maintenance and Repair of Stone Buildings, by D. G. Martin, ARIBA. 25p

Redecorating Your Church. 60p

Church Clocks. 7p

Monumental Brasses and Brass Rubbing. 20p

Brass Rubbing Licence. Per pad of 25, 50p

PROPERTY
Parish Trusts. 1½p (per 50 copies, 55p)

Notes for Sequestrators. (LF 4). 11p

Terrier and Inventory. (Combined and revised in 1972). £1.33

Church Log Book
Details of repairs and quinquennial inspections required to be kept by churchwardens under Canon F.13 (4). £1.53

STEWARDSHIP
Explaining Christian Stewardship, by E. J. N. Wallis. 15p

How to Help Your Church by Deed of Covenant. per 25, 30p

How to Run a PCC Covenant Scheme. 4p

Form of Deed of Covenant for PCCs
    Annual payments—blue paper—per 25 copies, 25p
    For revision of annual payments—green paper, per 25 copies, 30p
    For weekly payments—pink paper, per 25 copies, 25p
    For revision of weekly payments—yellow paper, per 25 copies, 30p

GENERAL INTEREST
Church of England Yearbook, 1974. £3.00 (published annually)

This list does not include reports on particular subjects under discussion to which reference may have been made in the book. The Synod continually has before it reports on matters of religious or social interest which are on sale to the public.

Index

This index is compiled primarily for practical use for lay officers. References which are unimportant or repetitive may be omitted and entries of general interest only are kept within reasonable compass. For Measures or Canons in operation reference should be made to their subject matter.

NOTES